THE
HAPPY GEEK'S
COLORING BOOK

Jaleh Afshar & Colleen Palmer

First edition: February 2016

ISBN-13: 978-1523868575

ISBN-10: 1523868570

happygeekscoloringbook.com

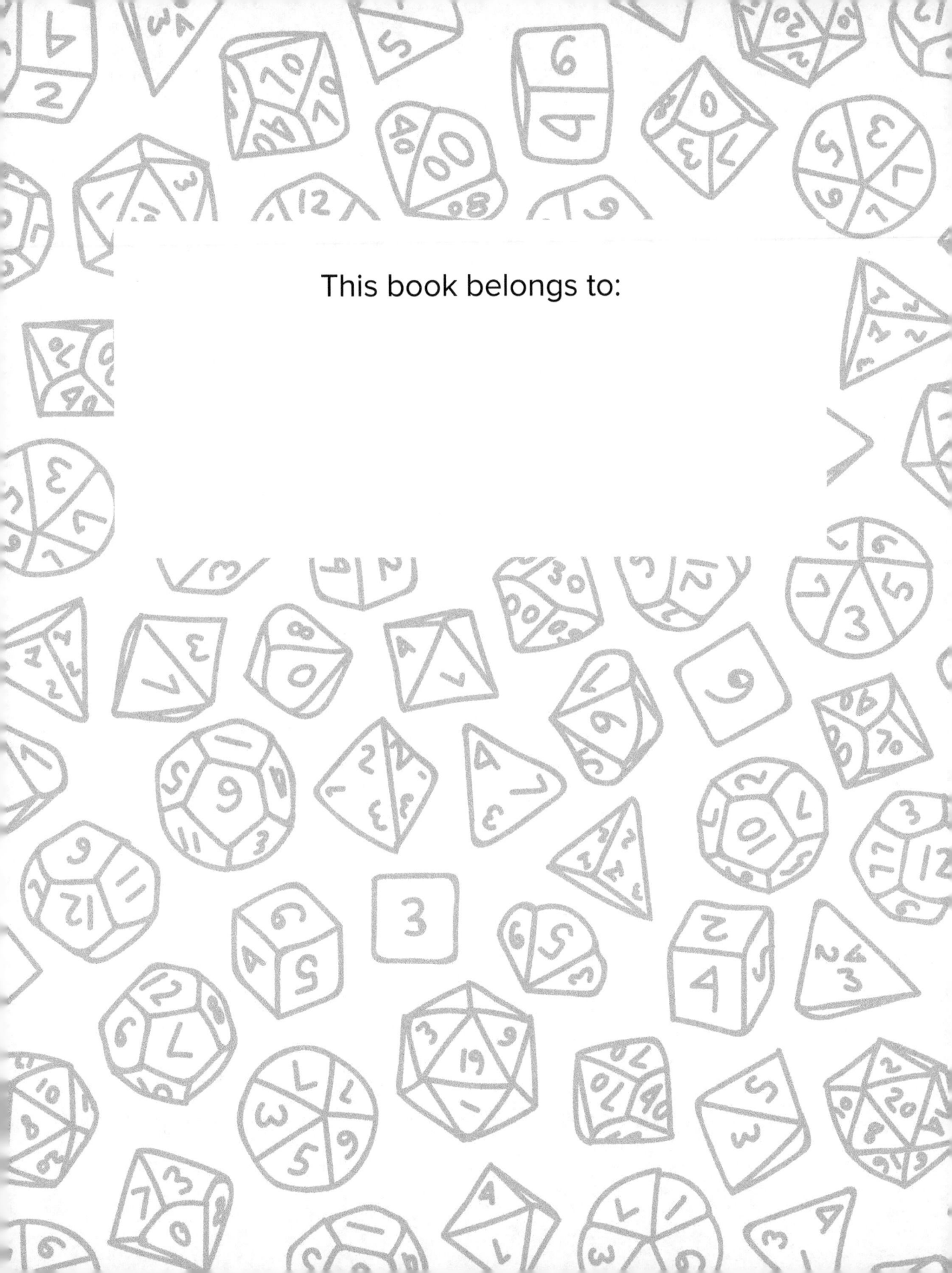

This book belongs to:

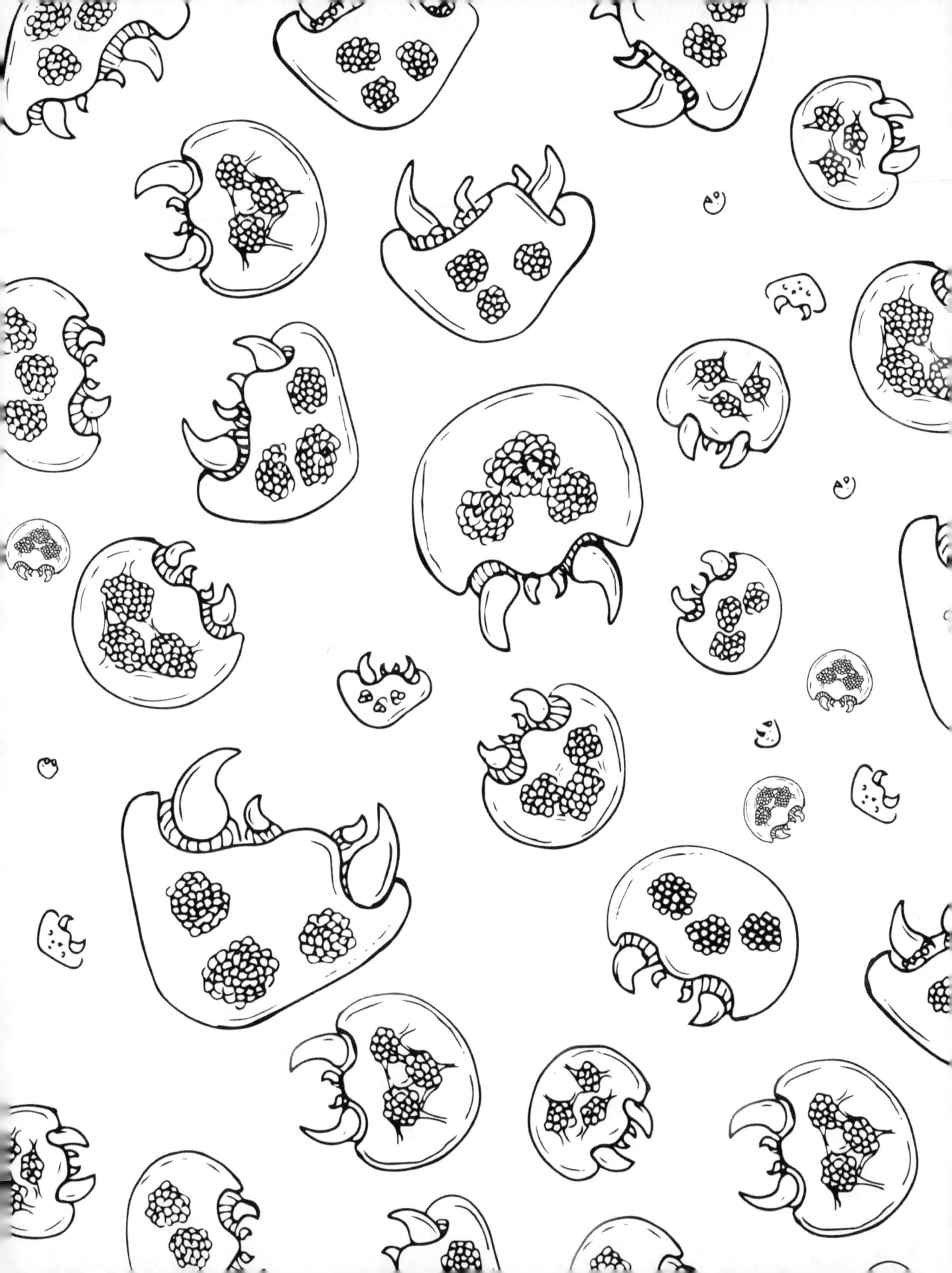

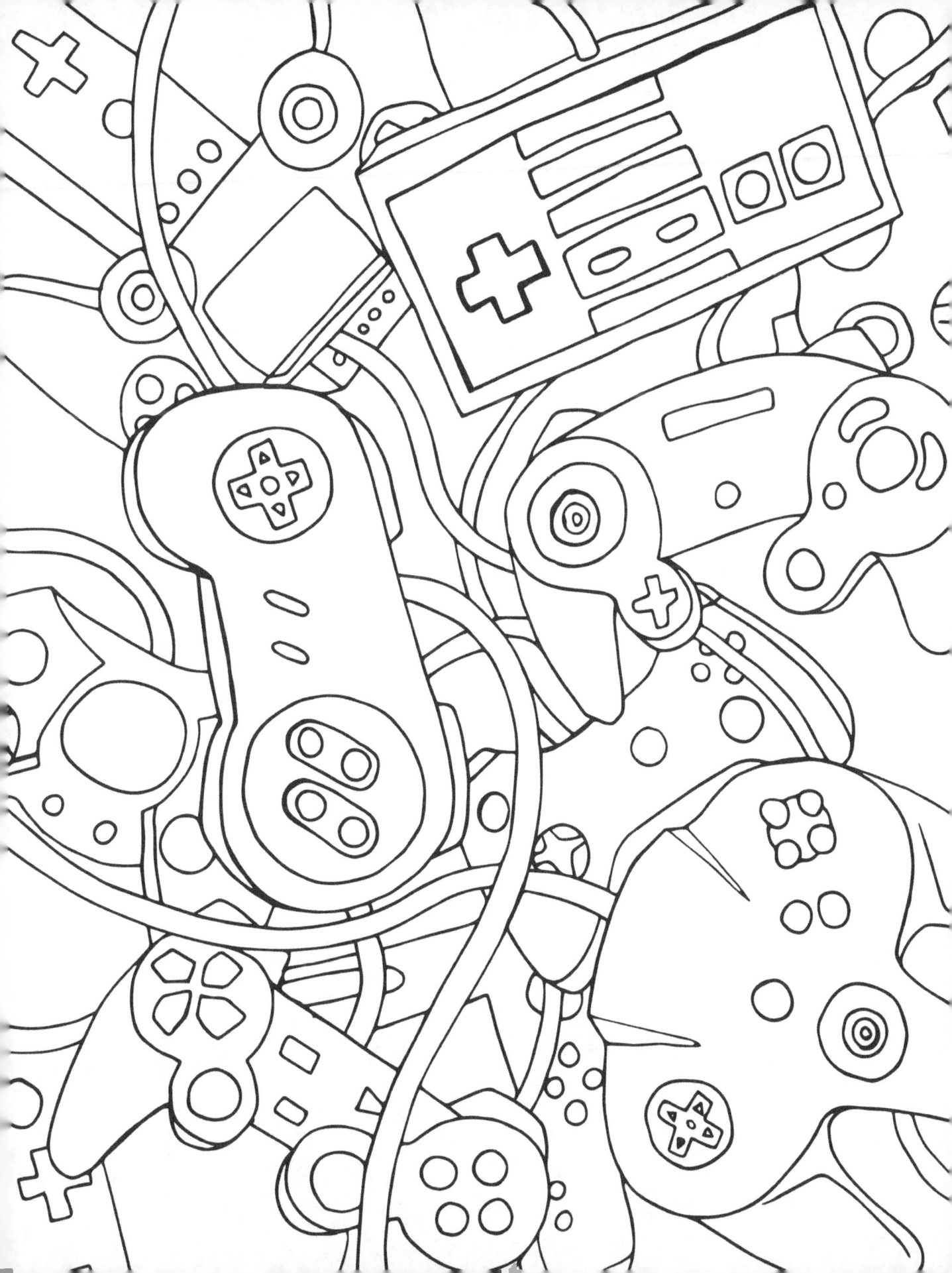

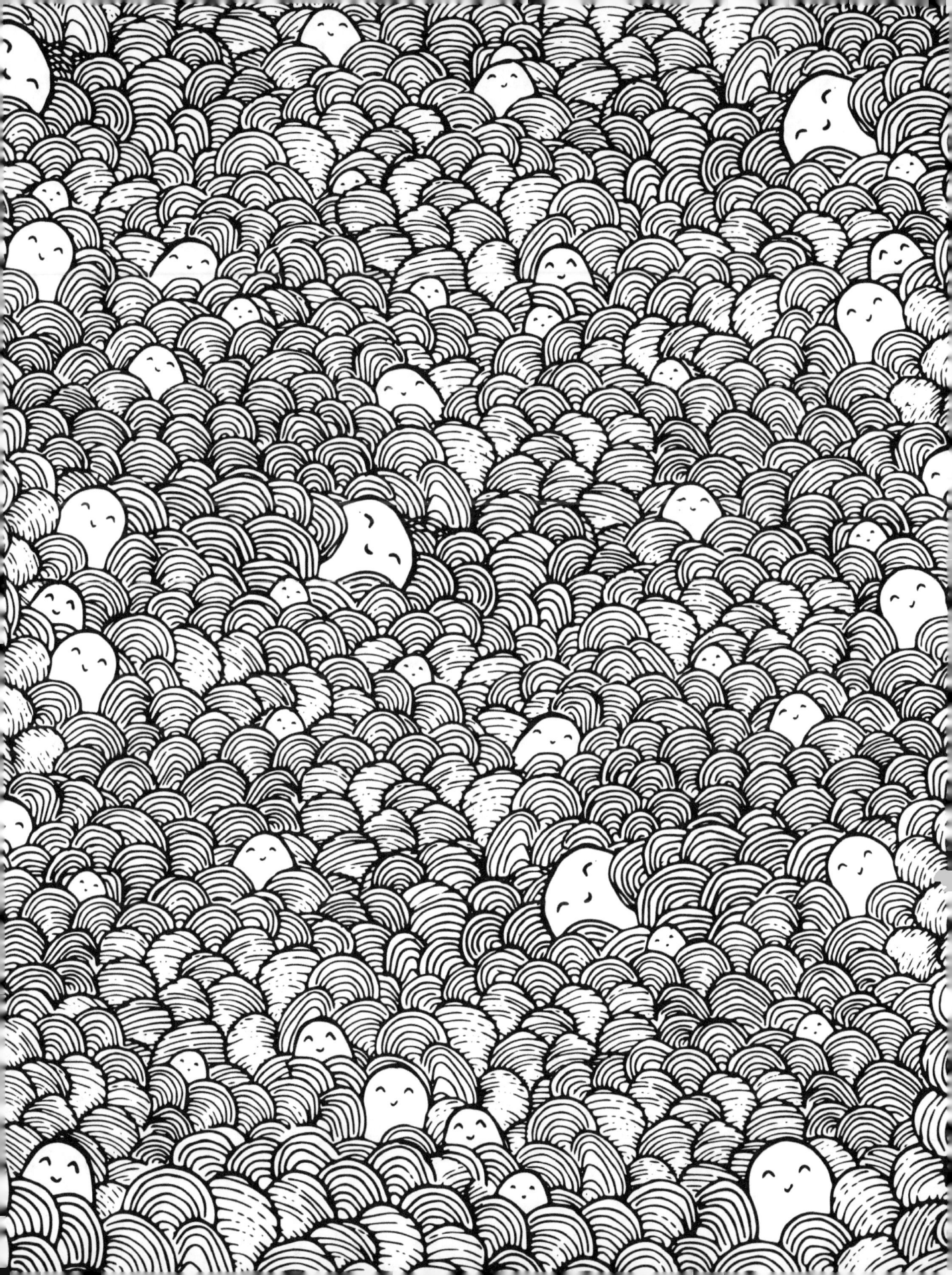

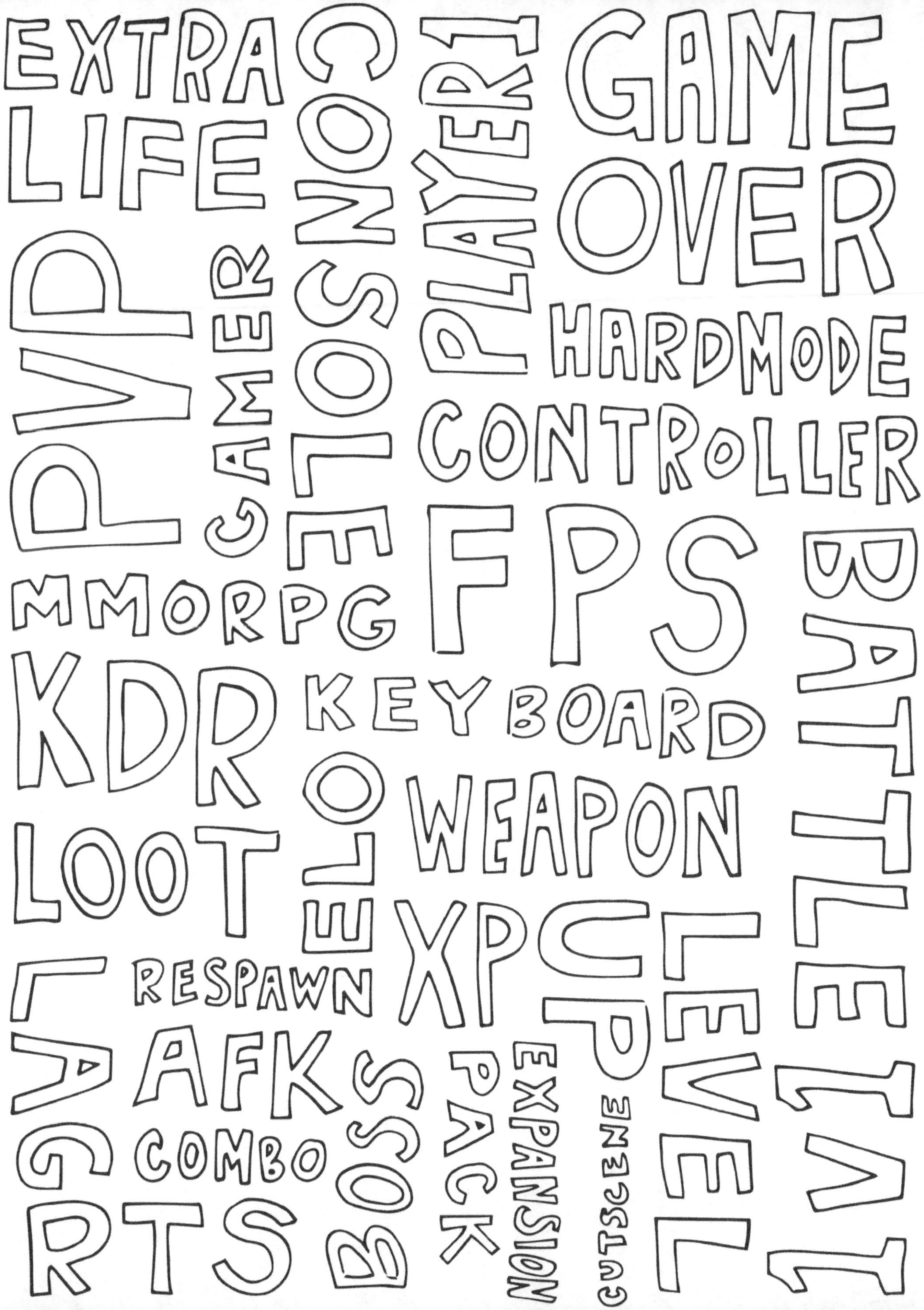

EXTRA LIFE

CONSOLE

PLAYER 1

GAME OVER

HARD MODE

CONTROLLER

GAMER

PVP

FPS

BATTLE

MMORPG

KDR

KEYBOARD

LOOT

WEAPON

TELEPORT

XP

LEVEL UP

LAG

RESPAWN

AFK

BOSS

EXPANSION PACK

CUTSCENE

COMBO

RTS

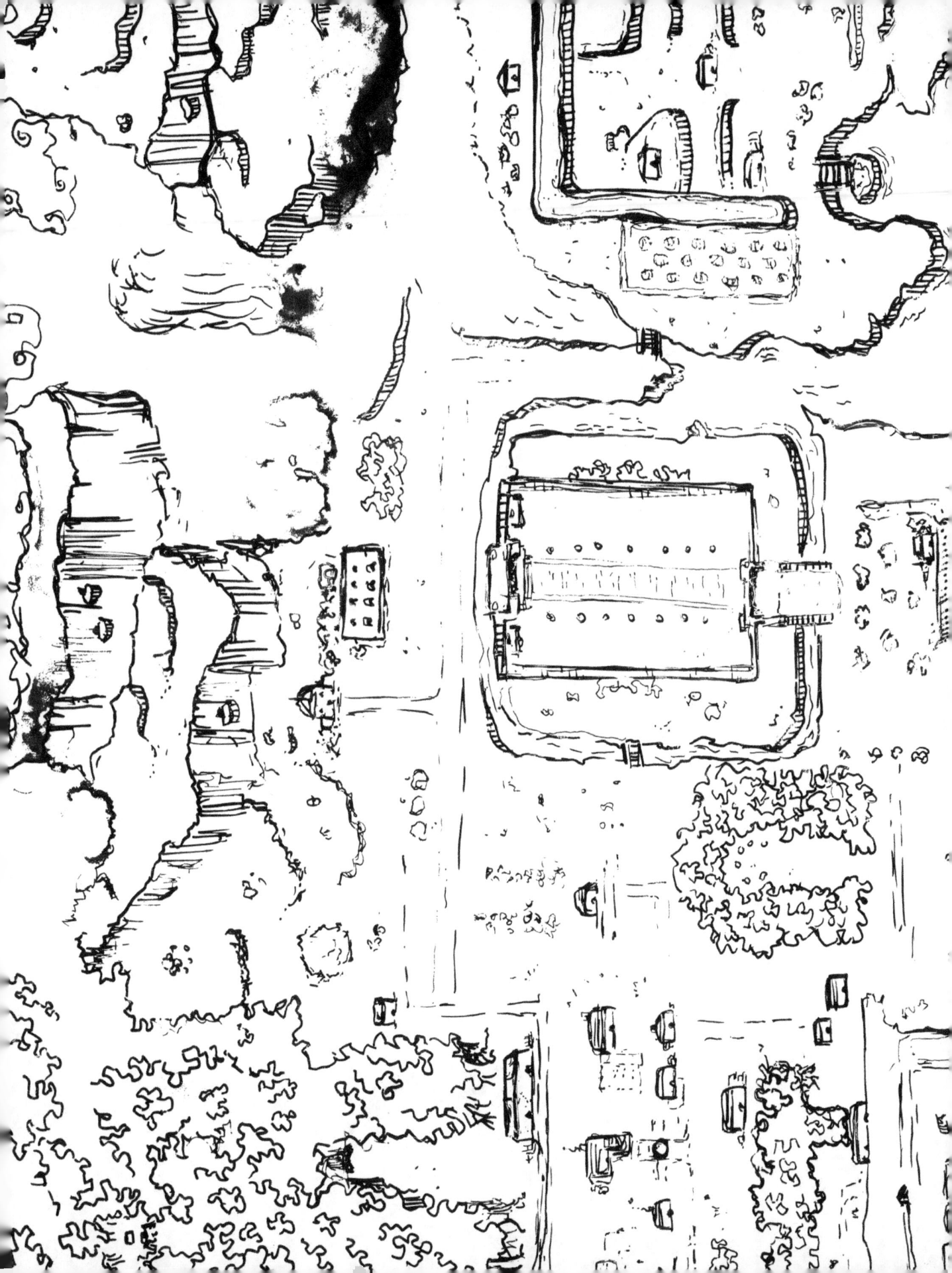

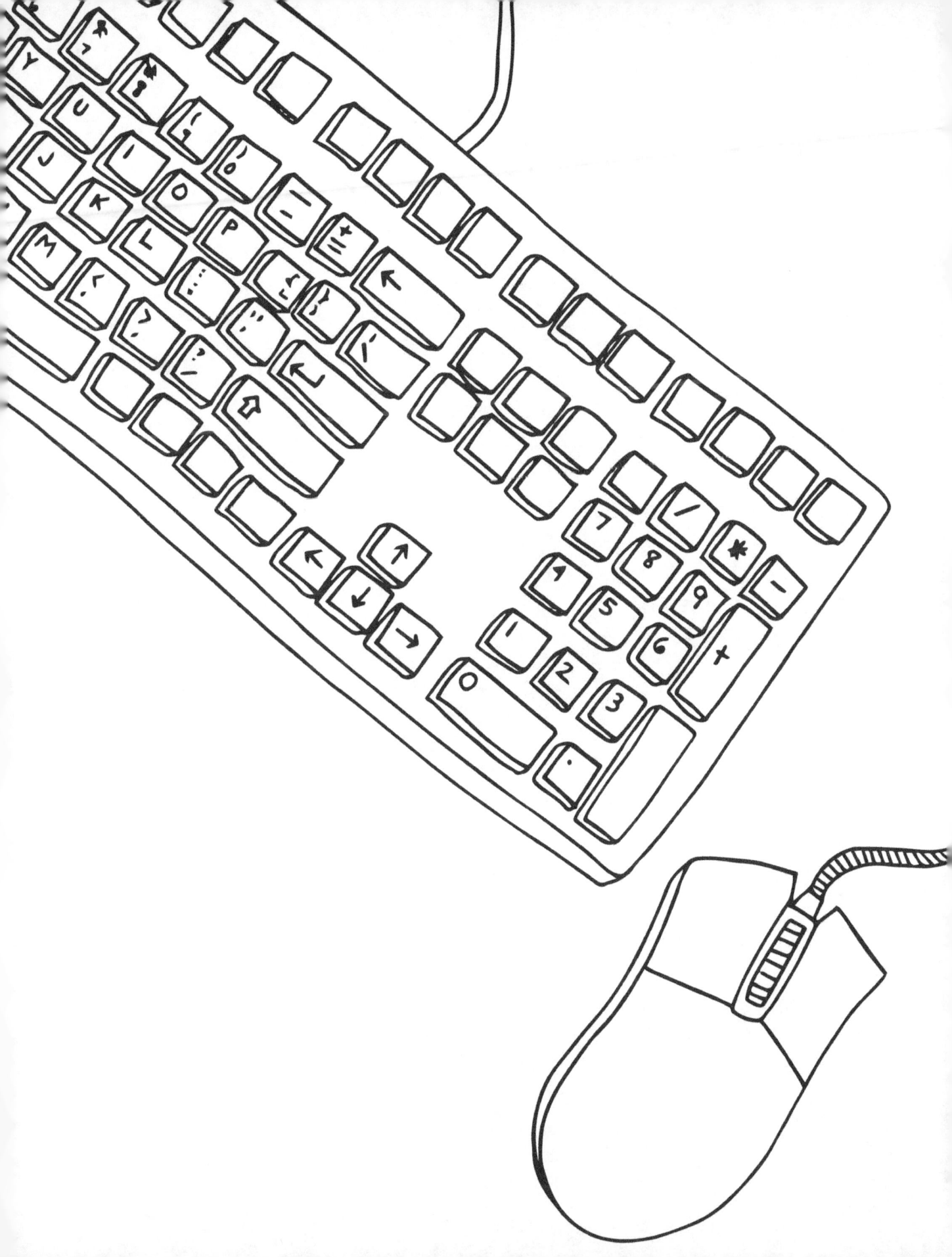

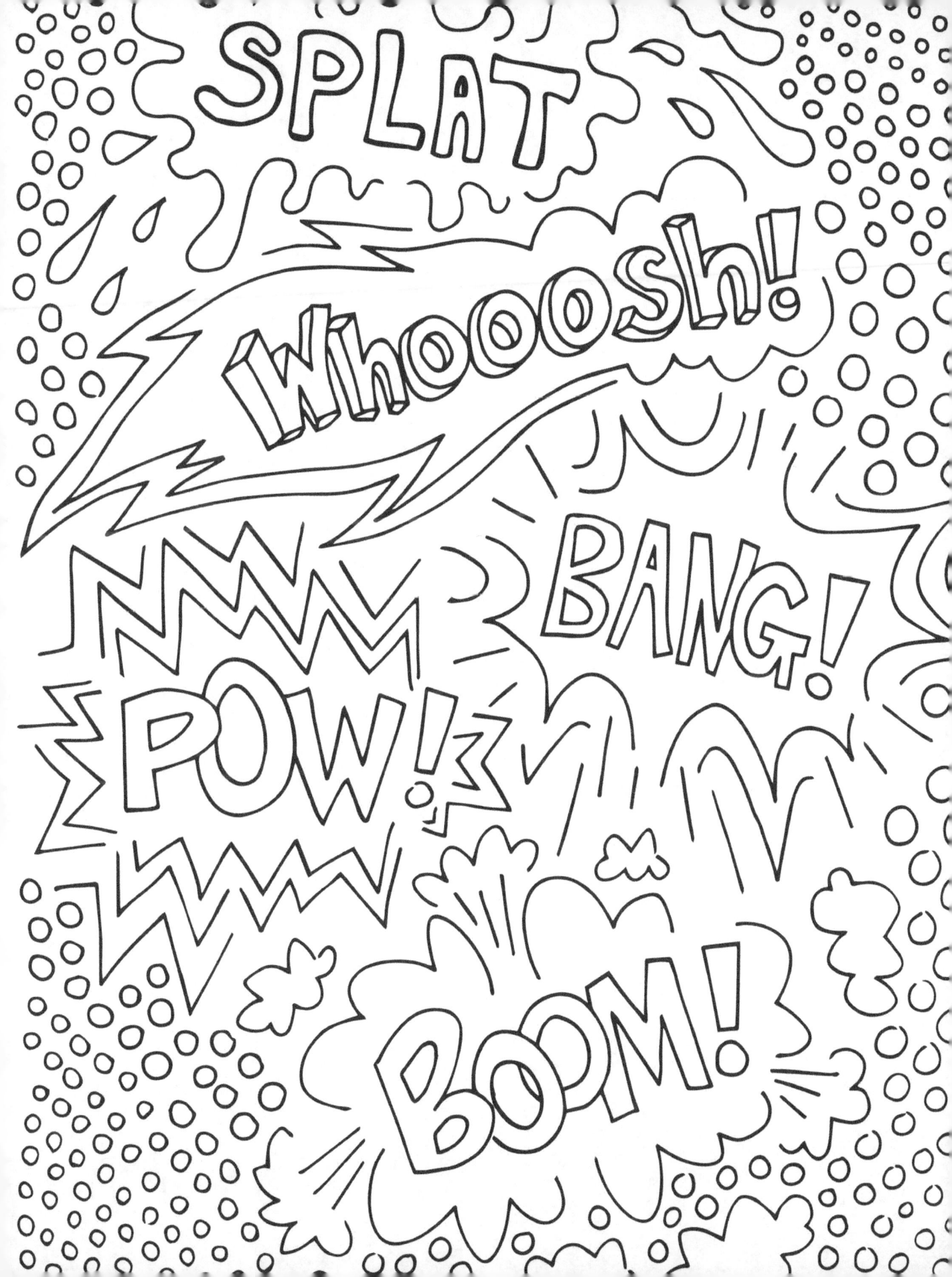

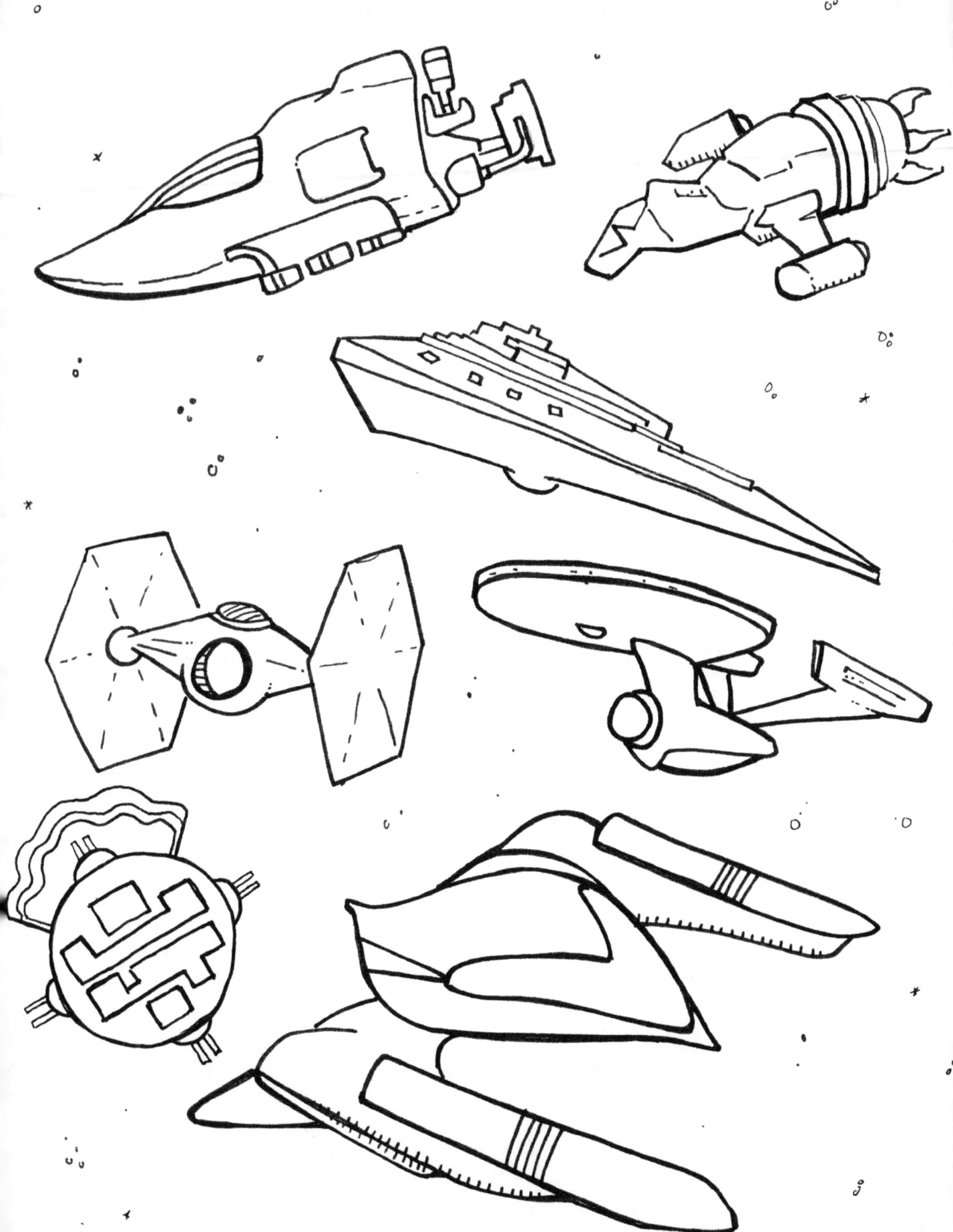

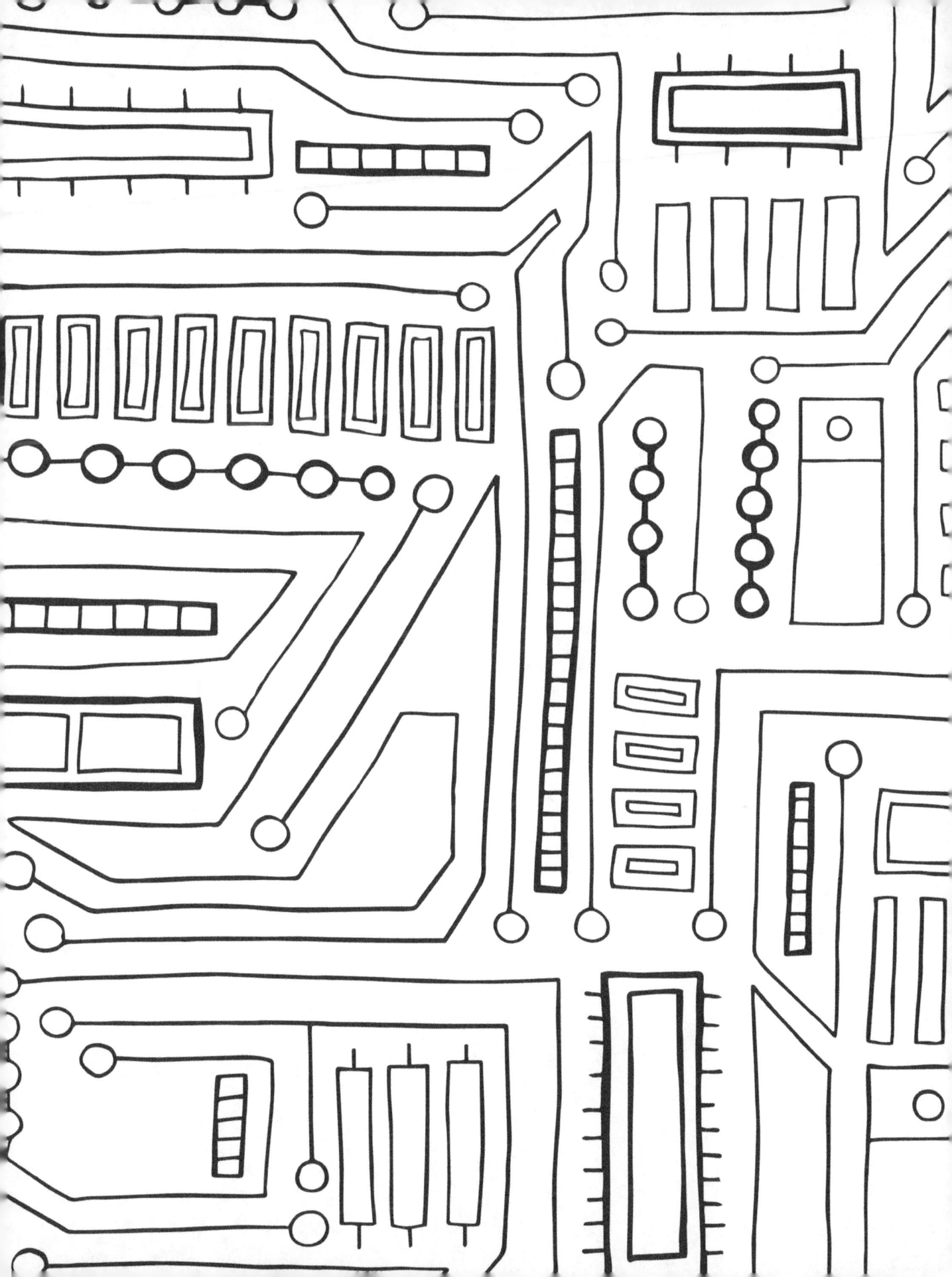

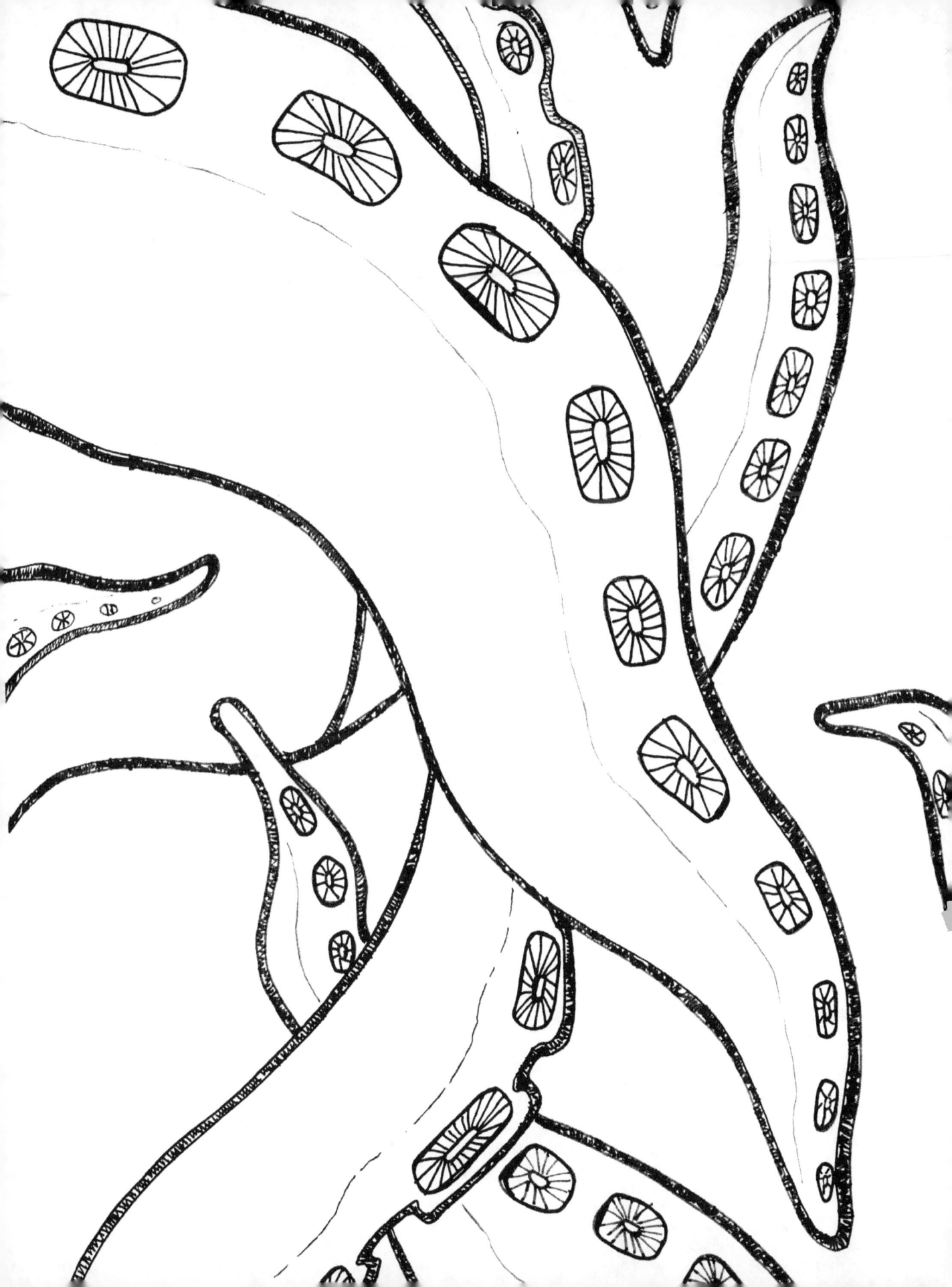

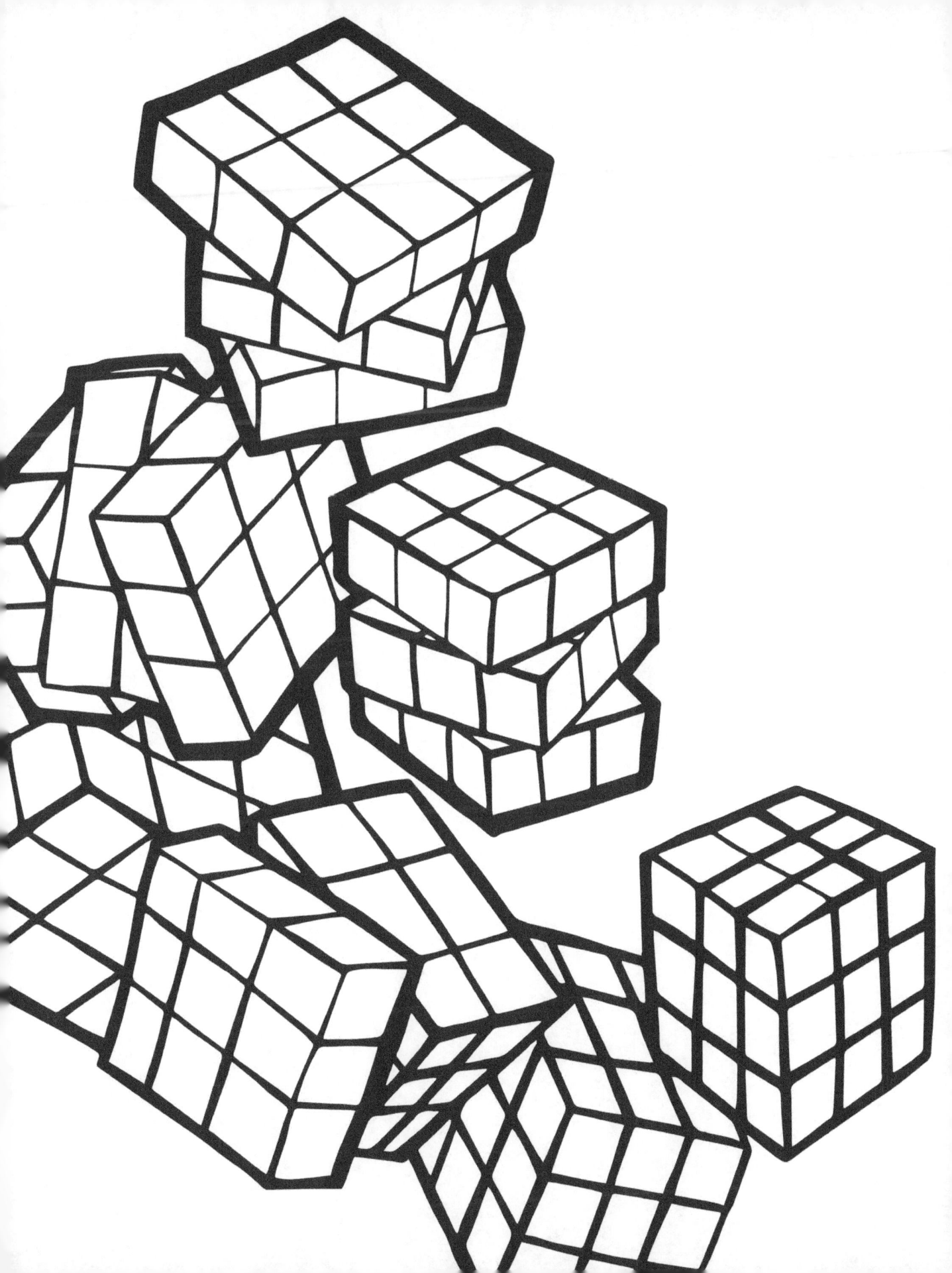

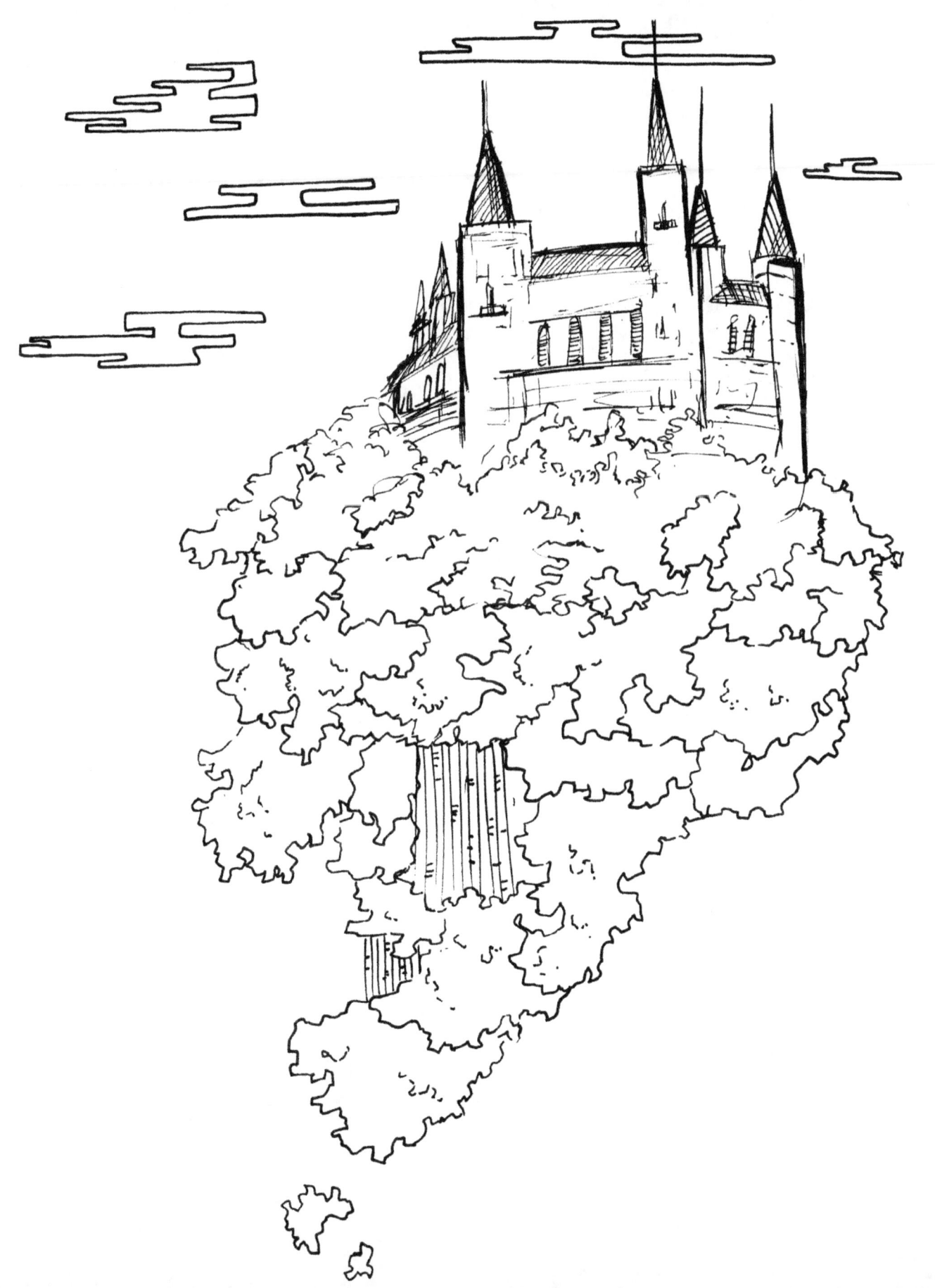

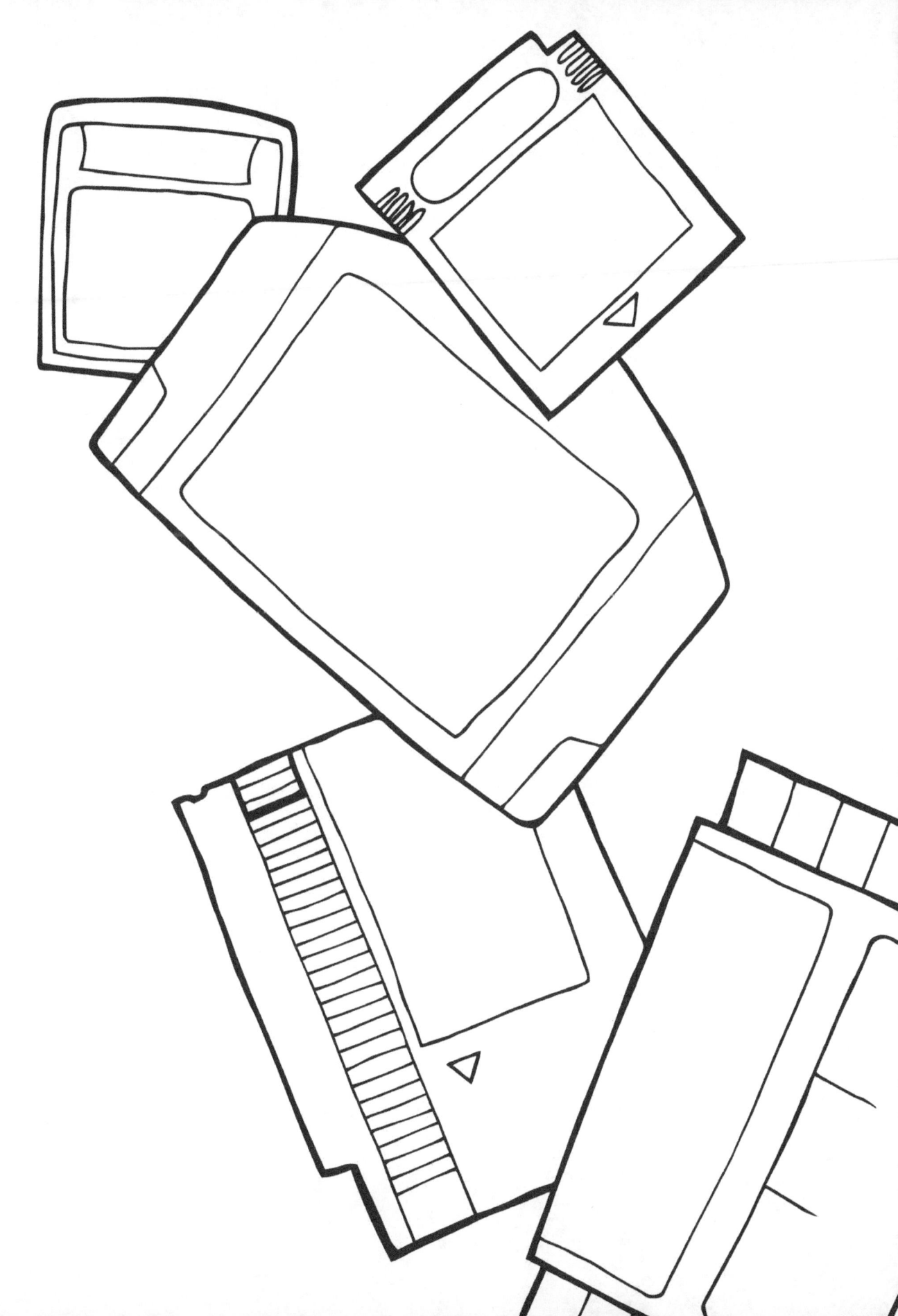

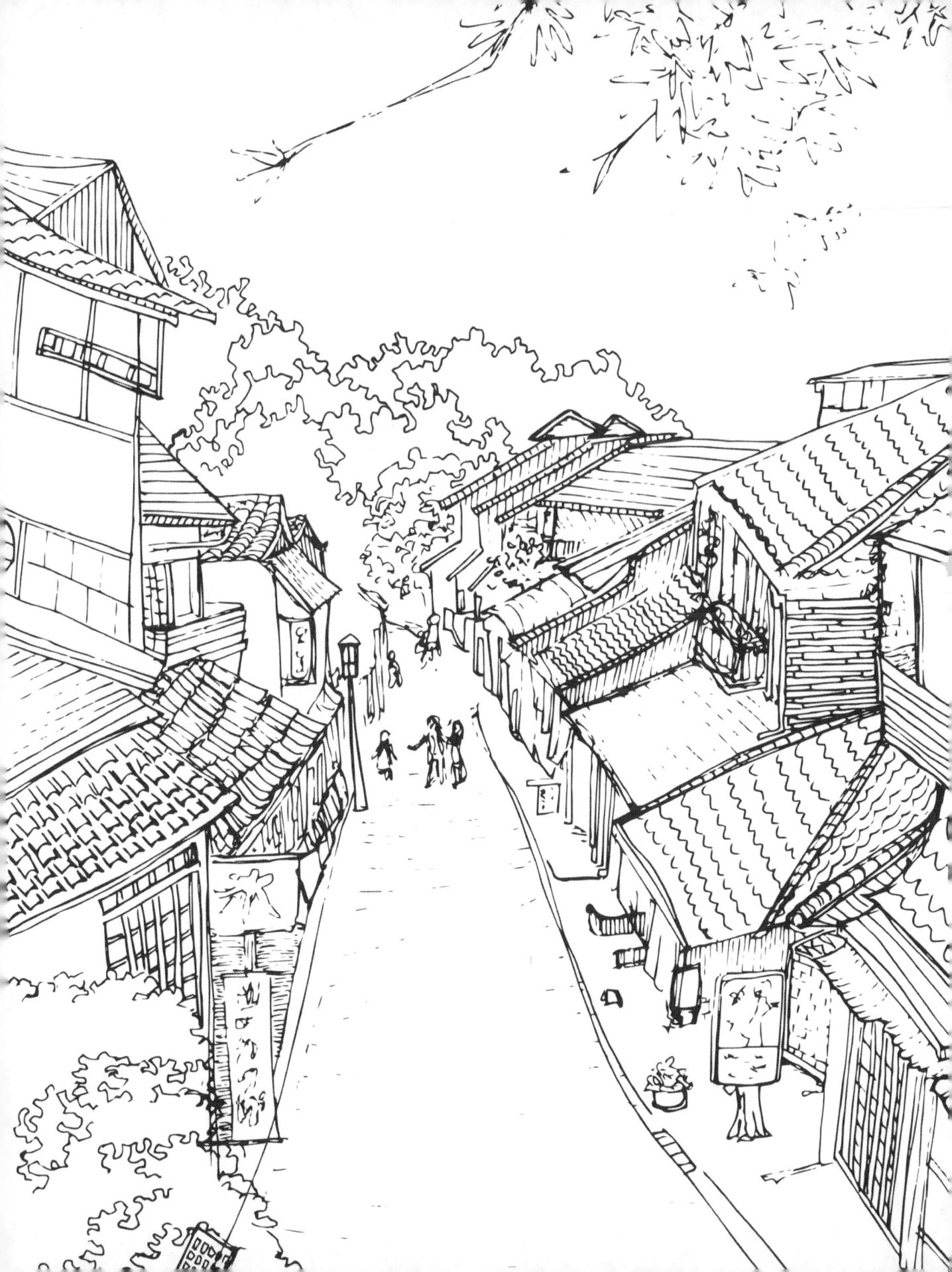

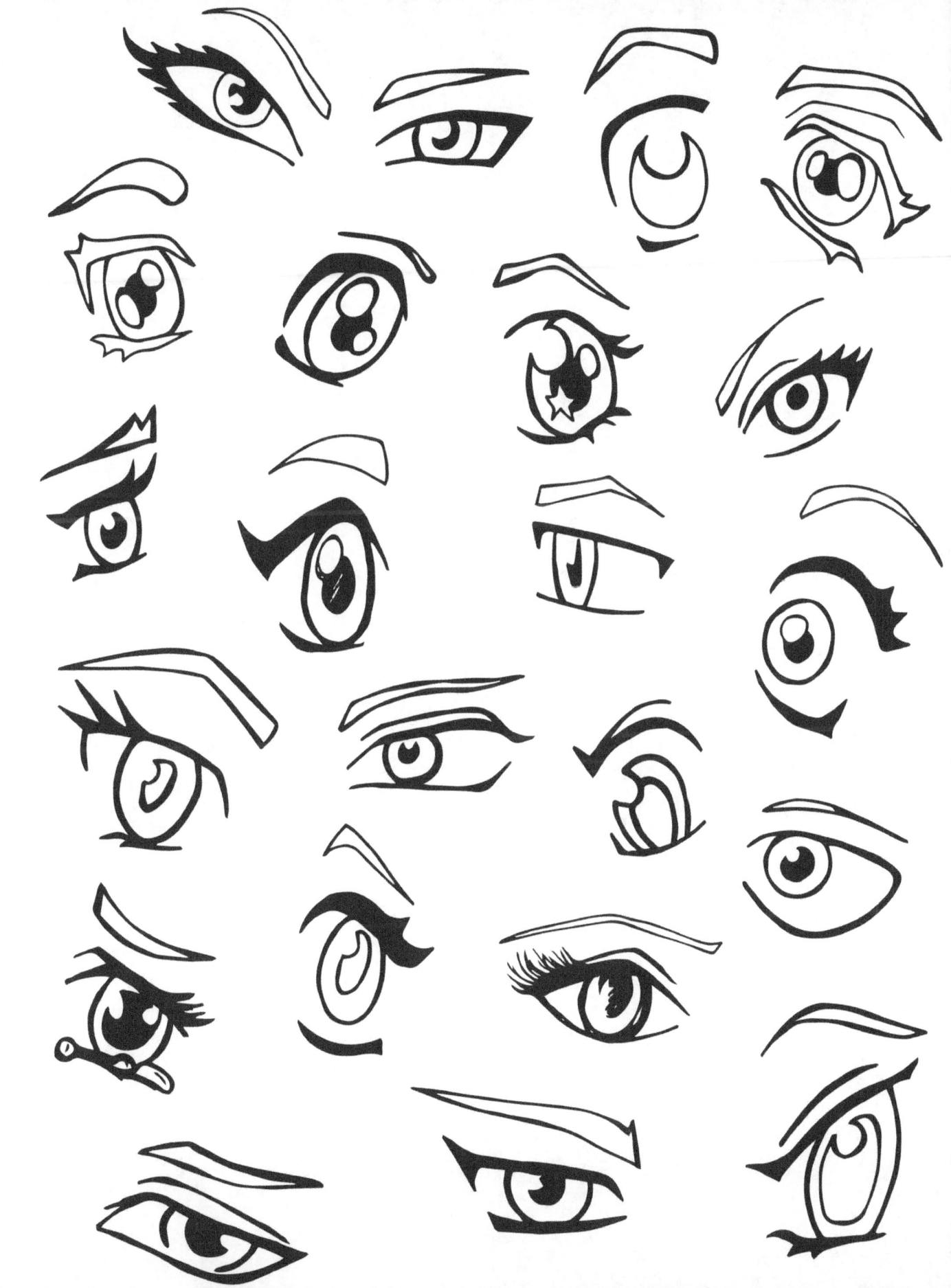

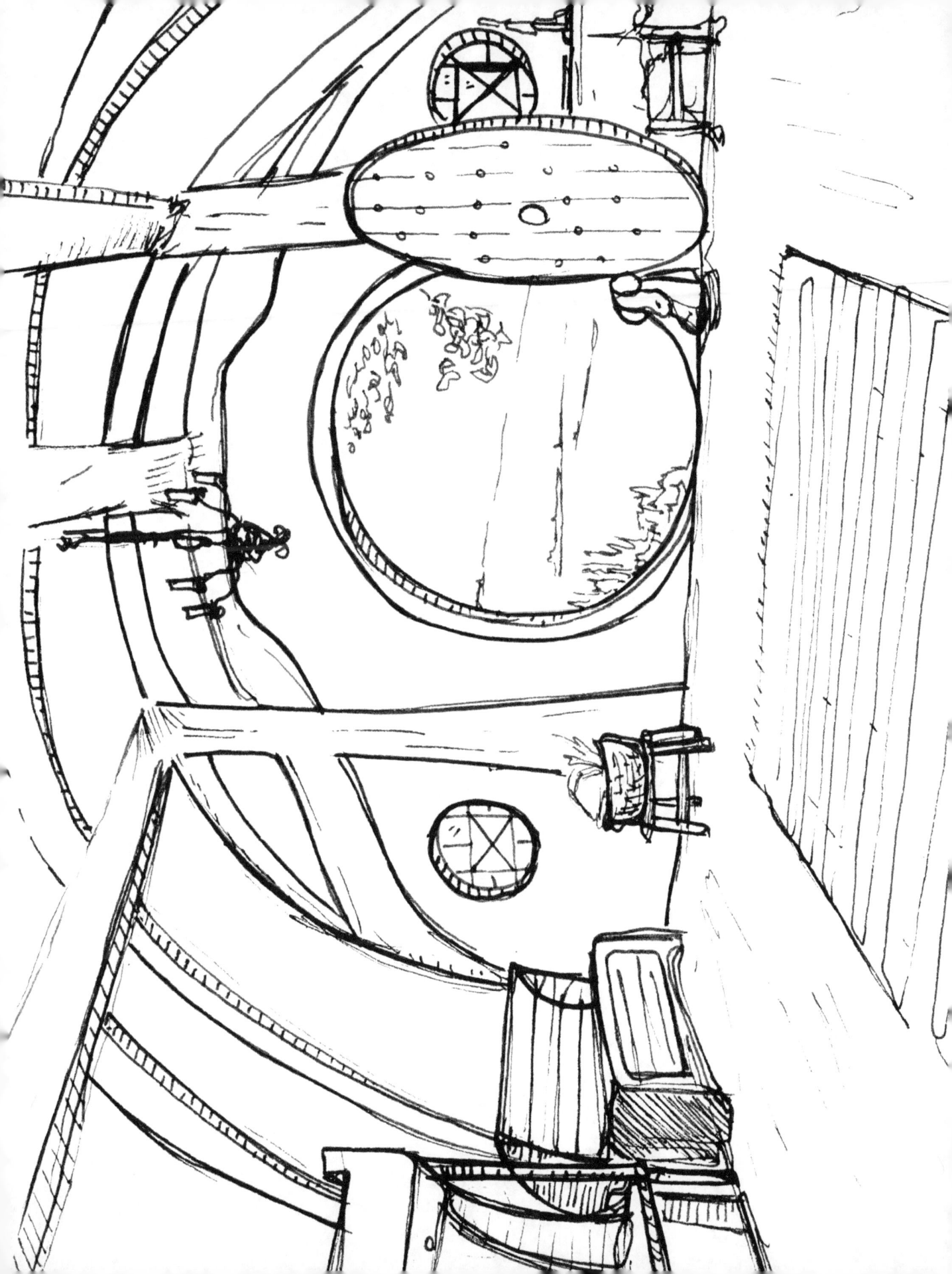

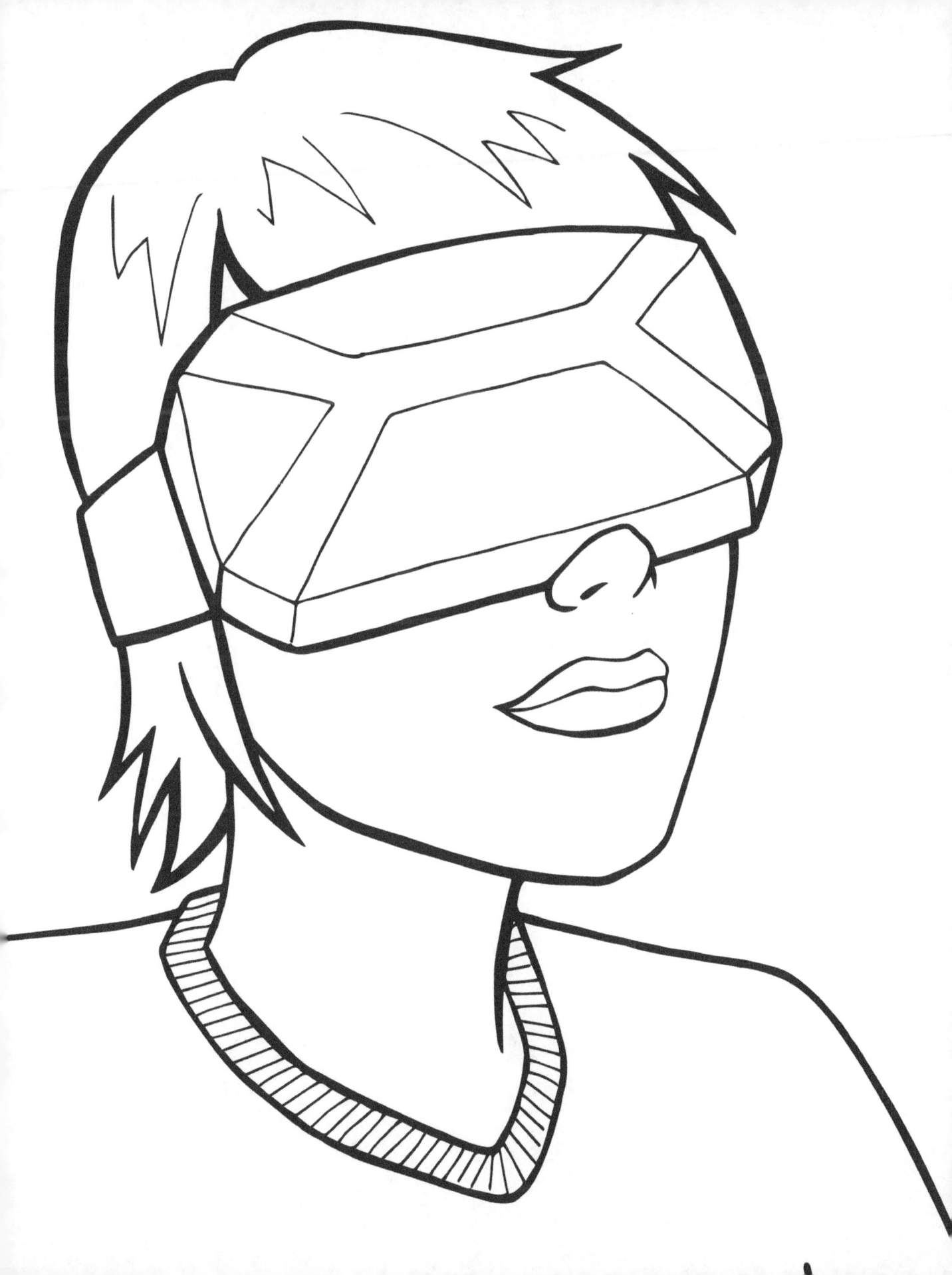

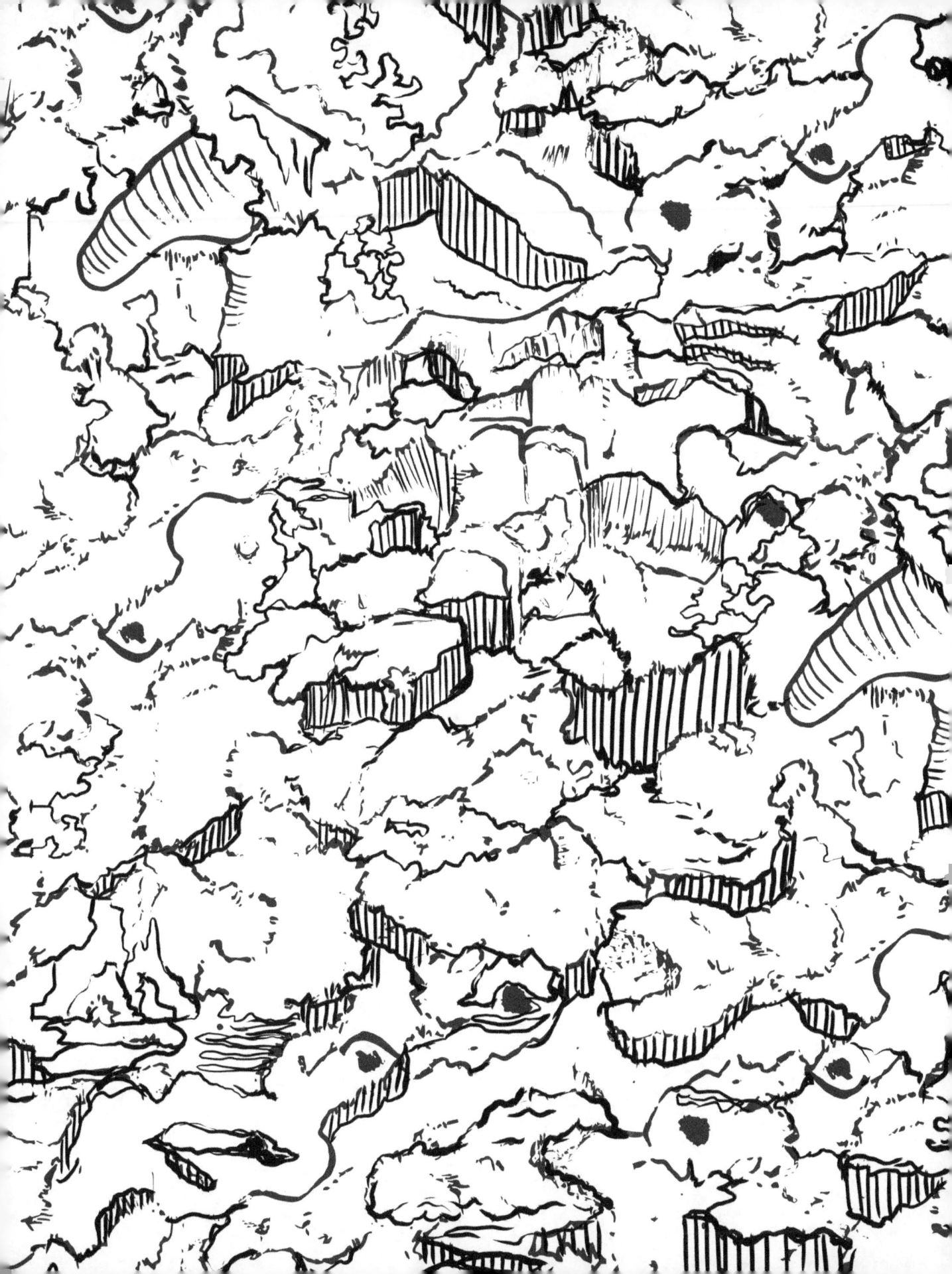

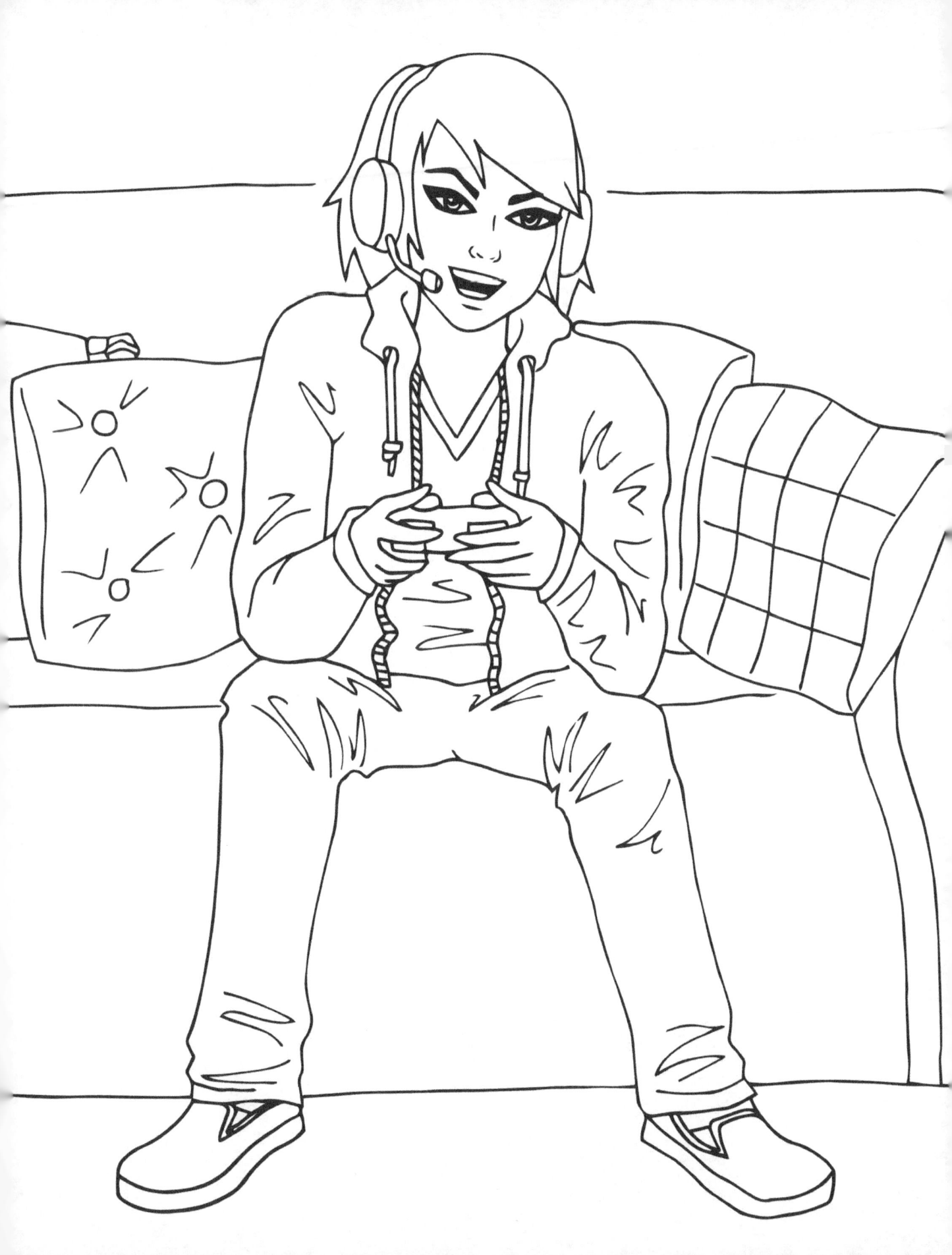

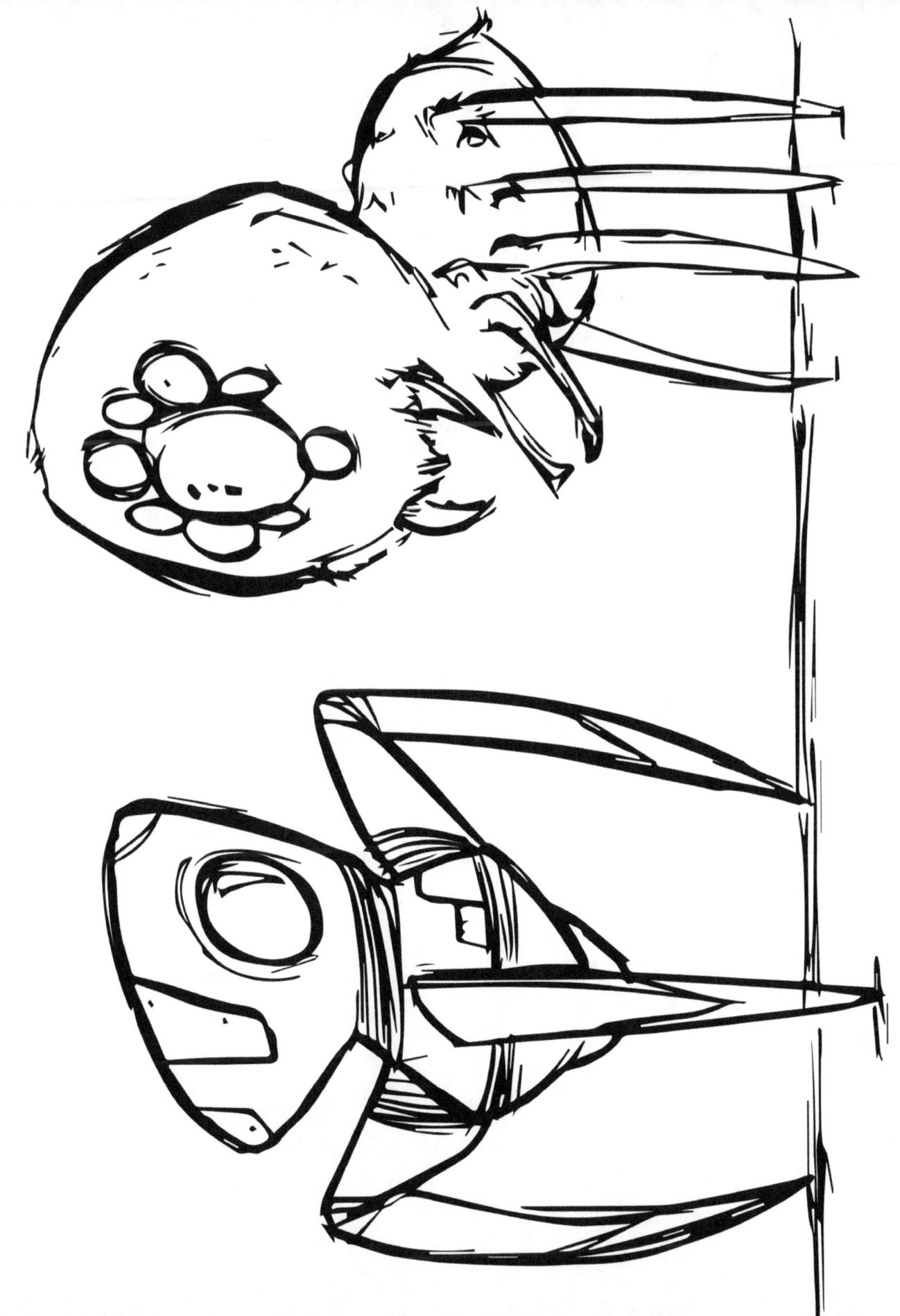

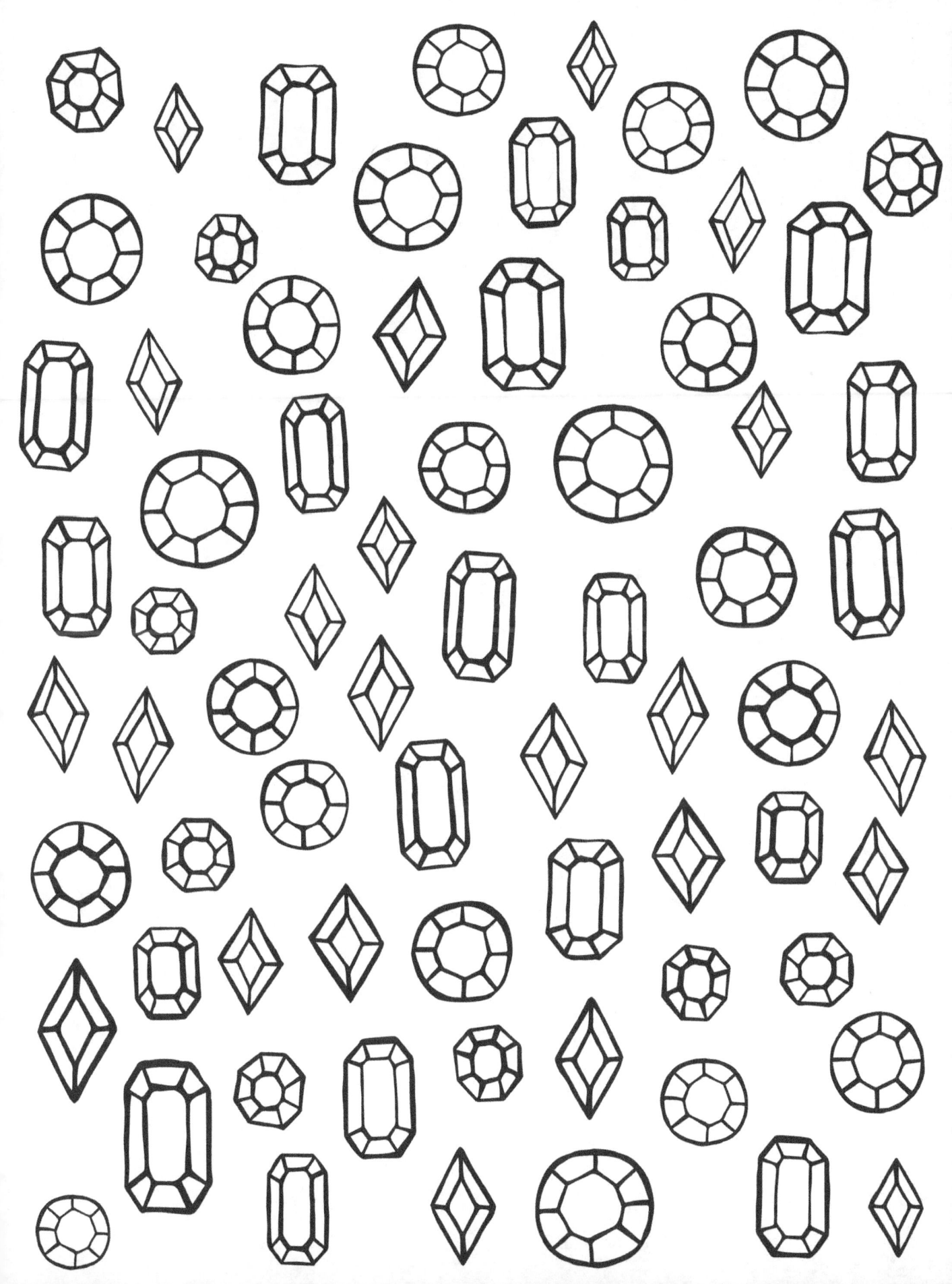

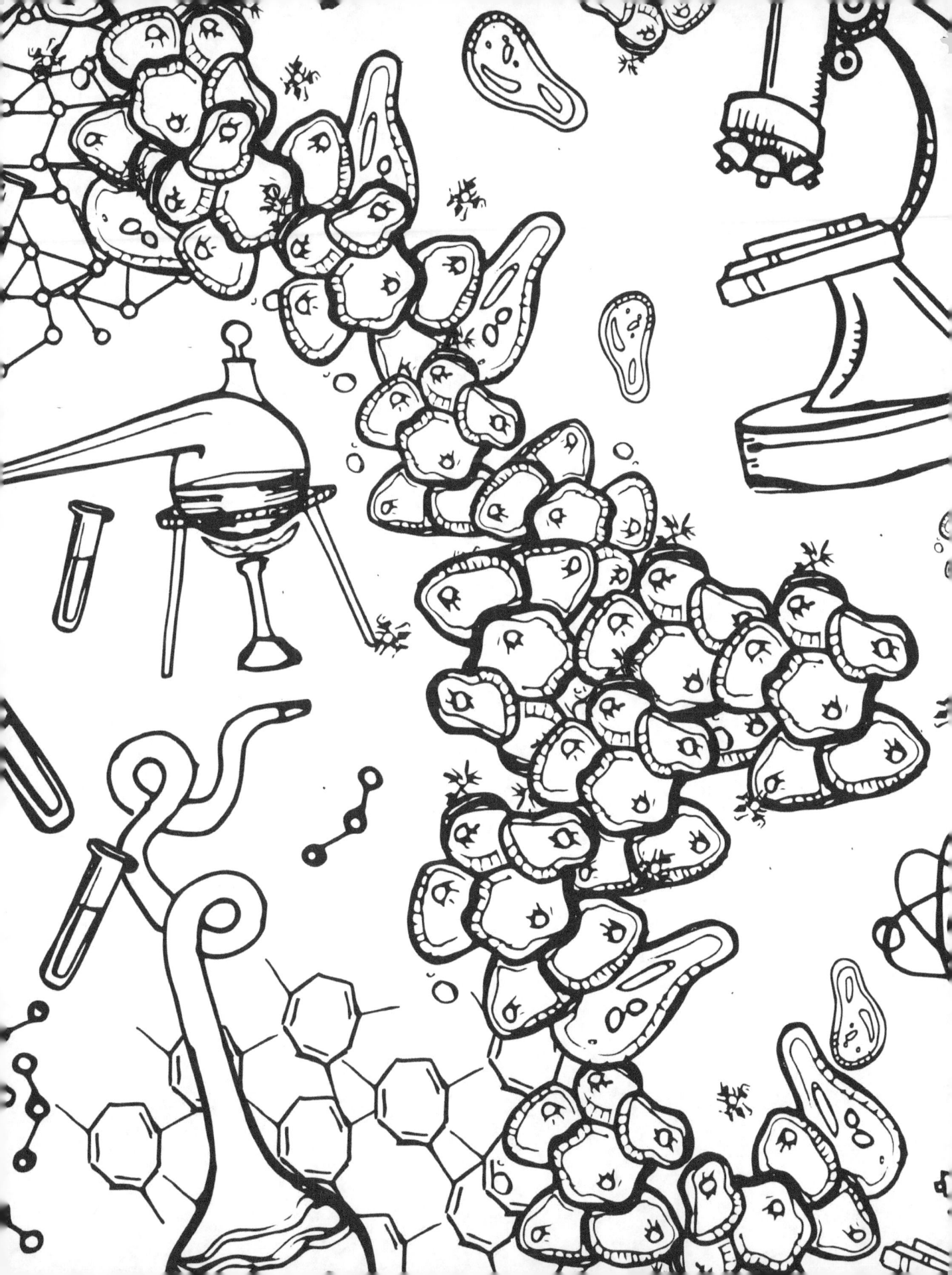

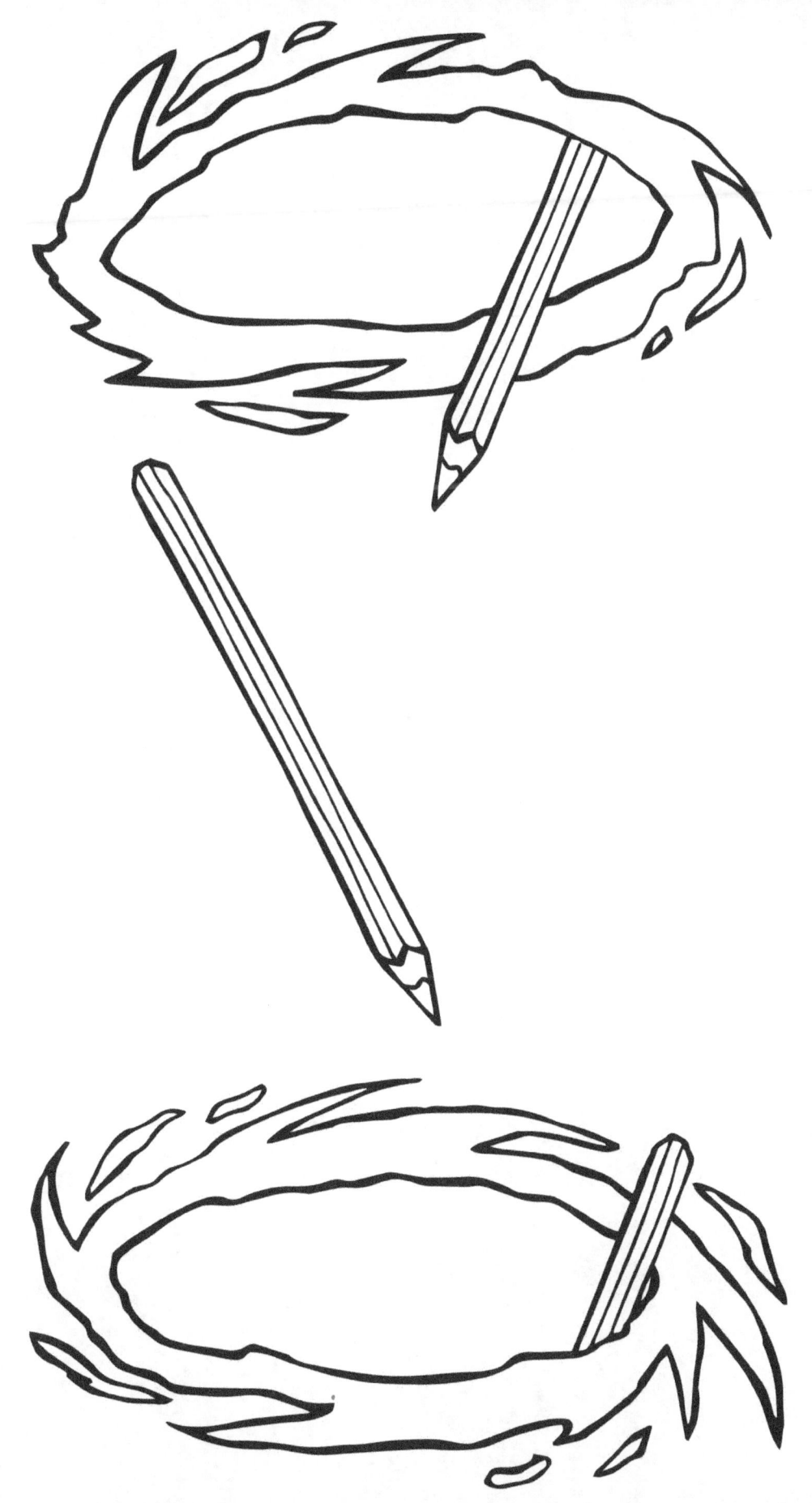

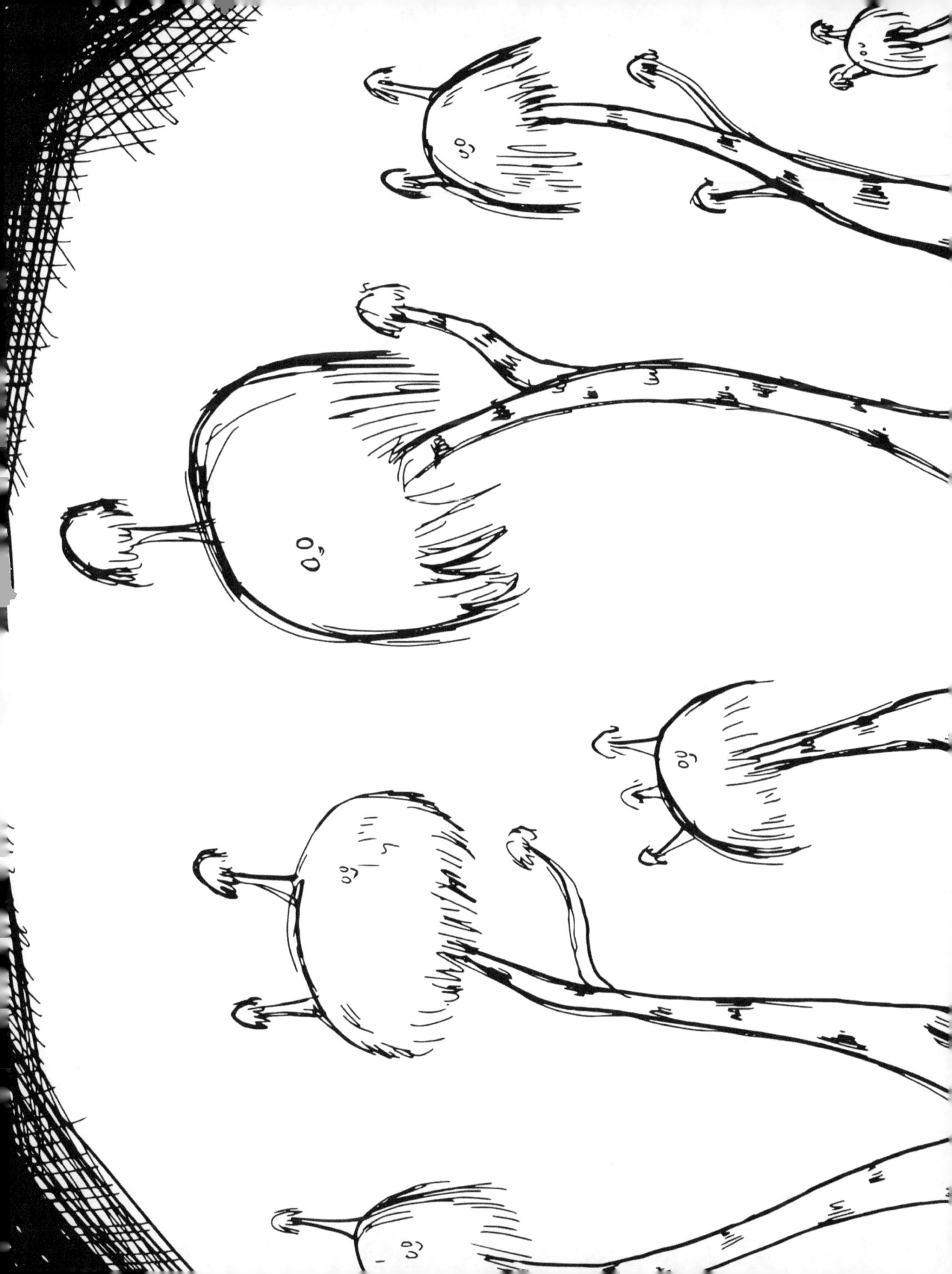

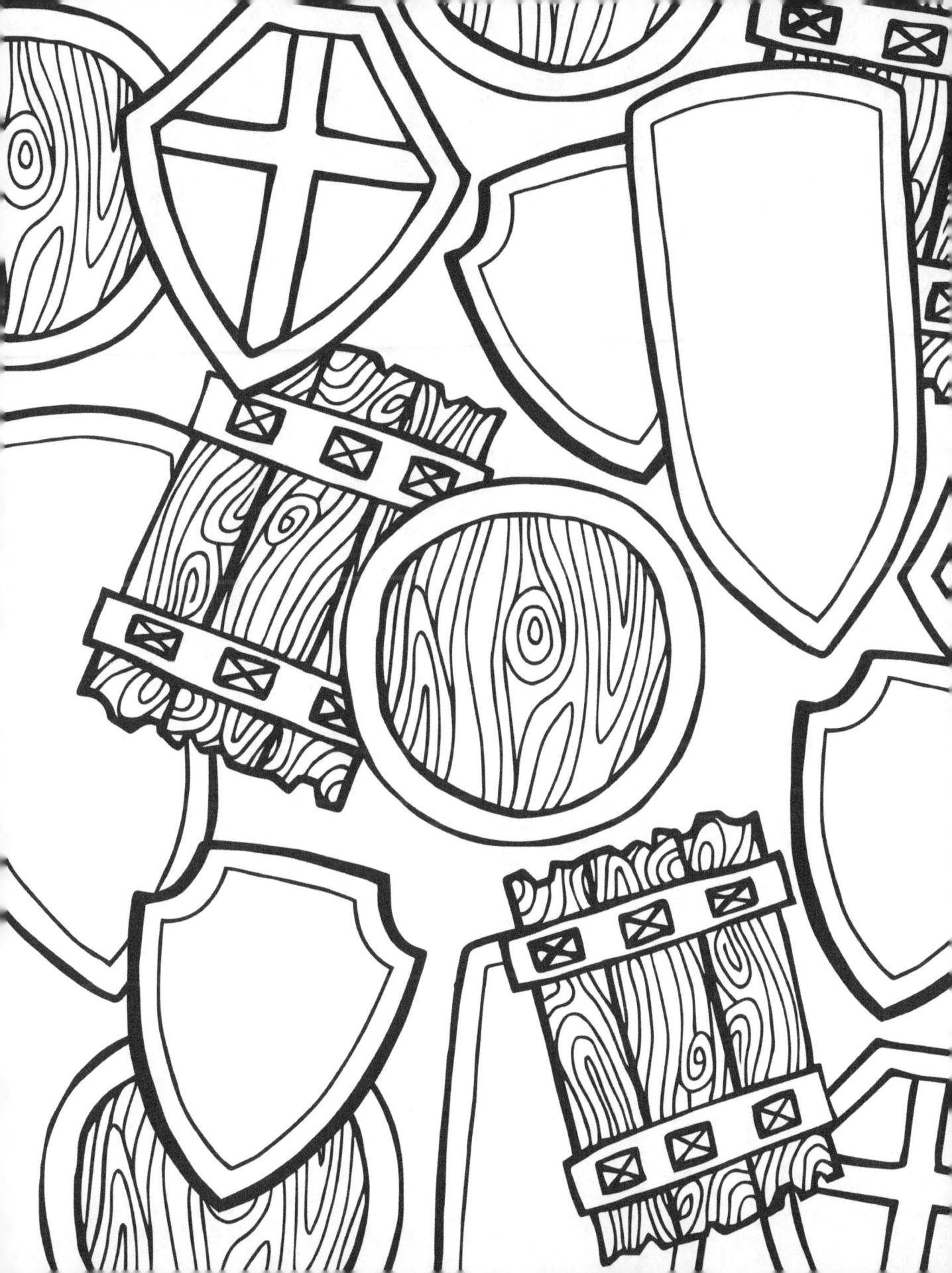

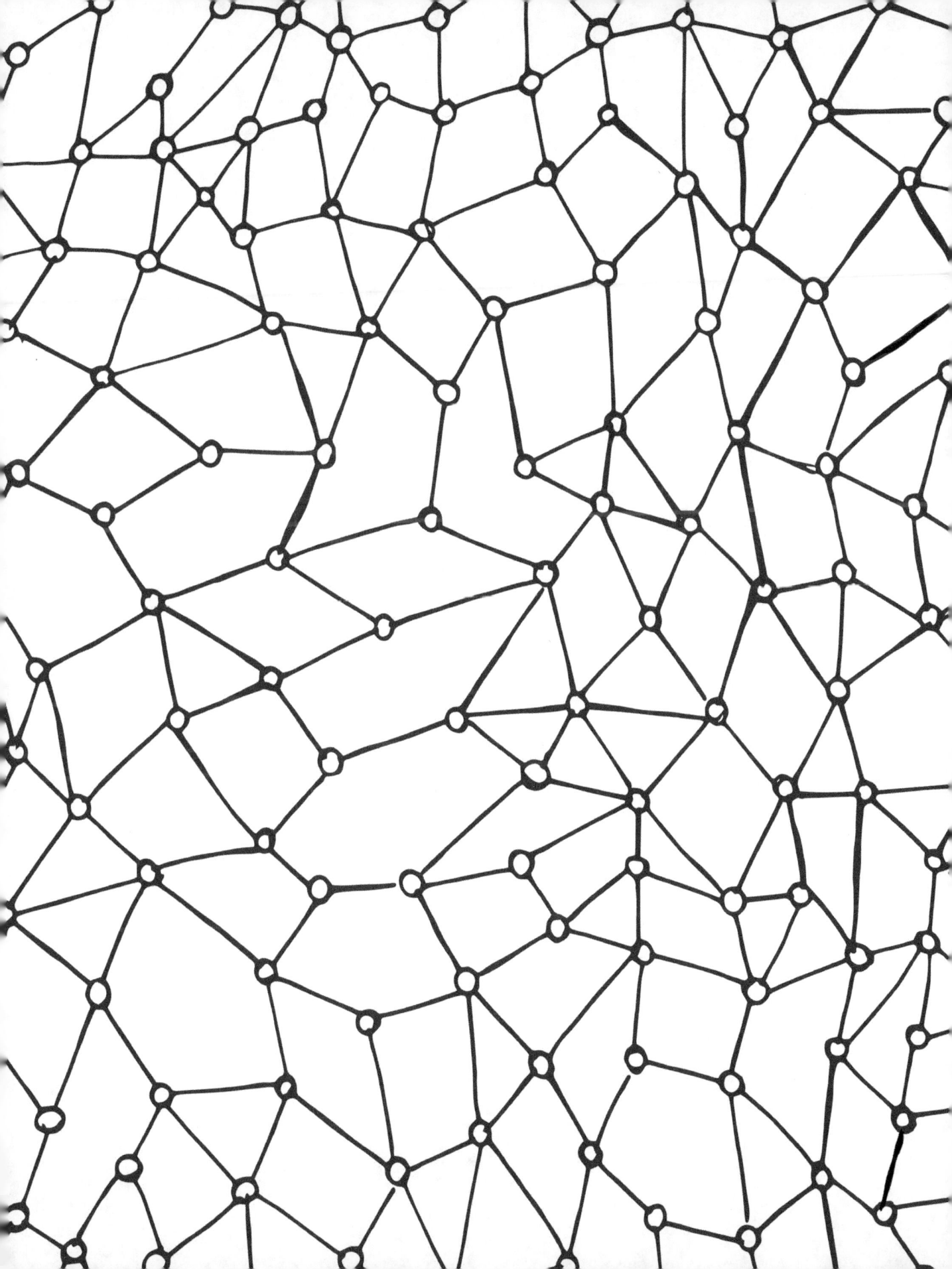

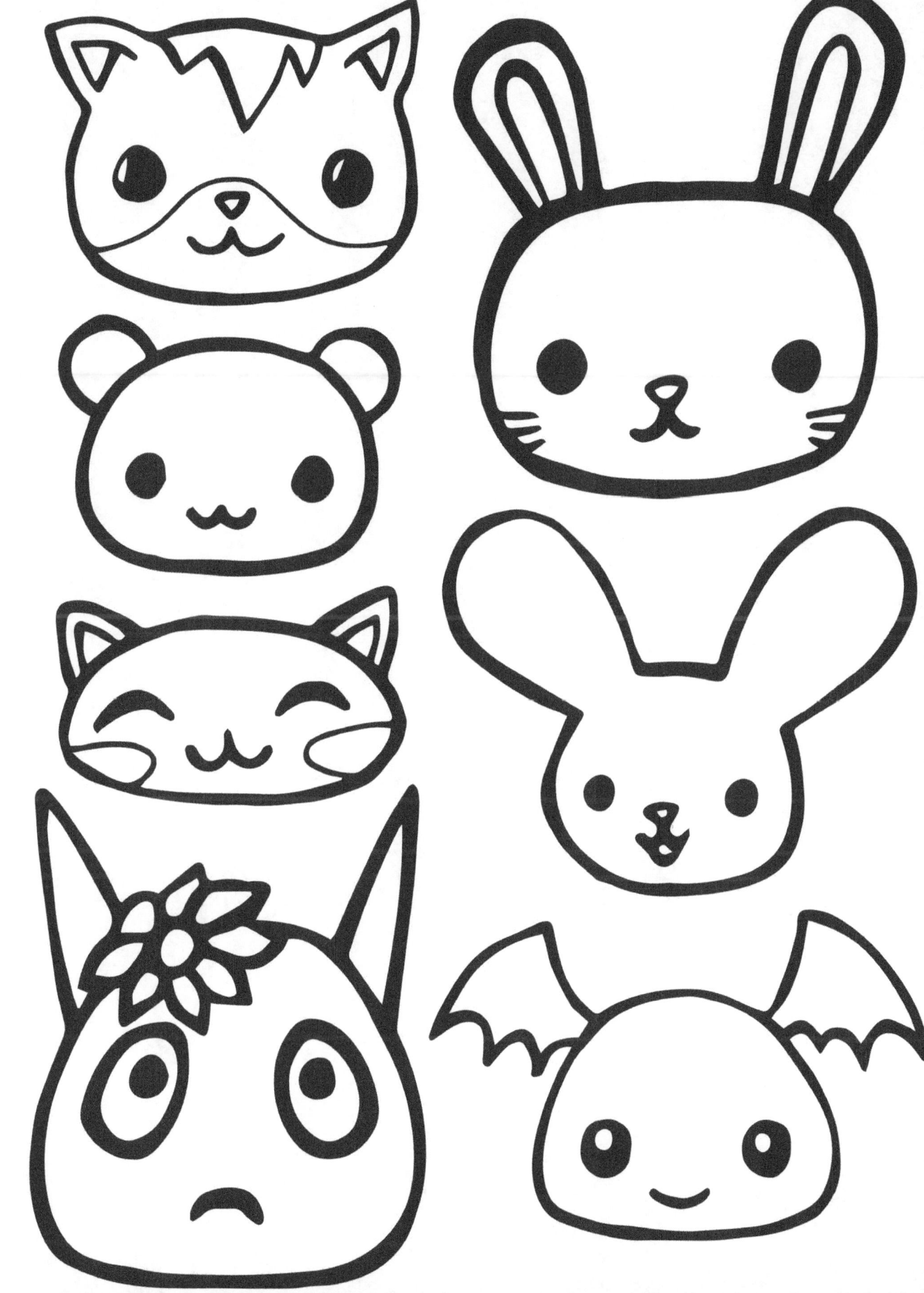

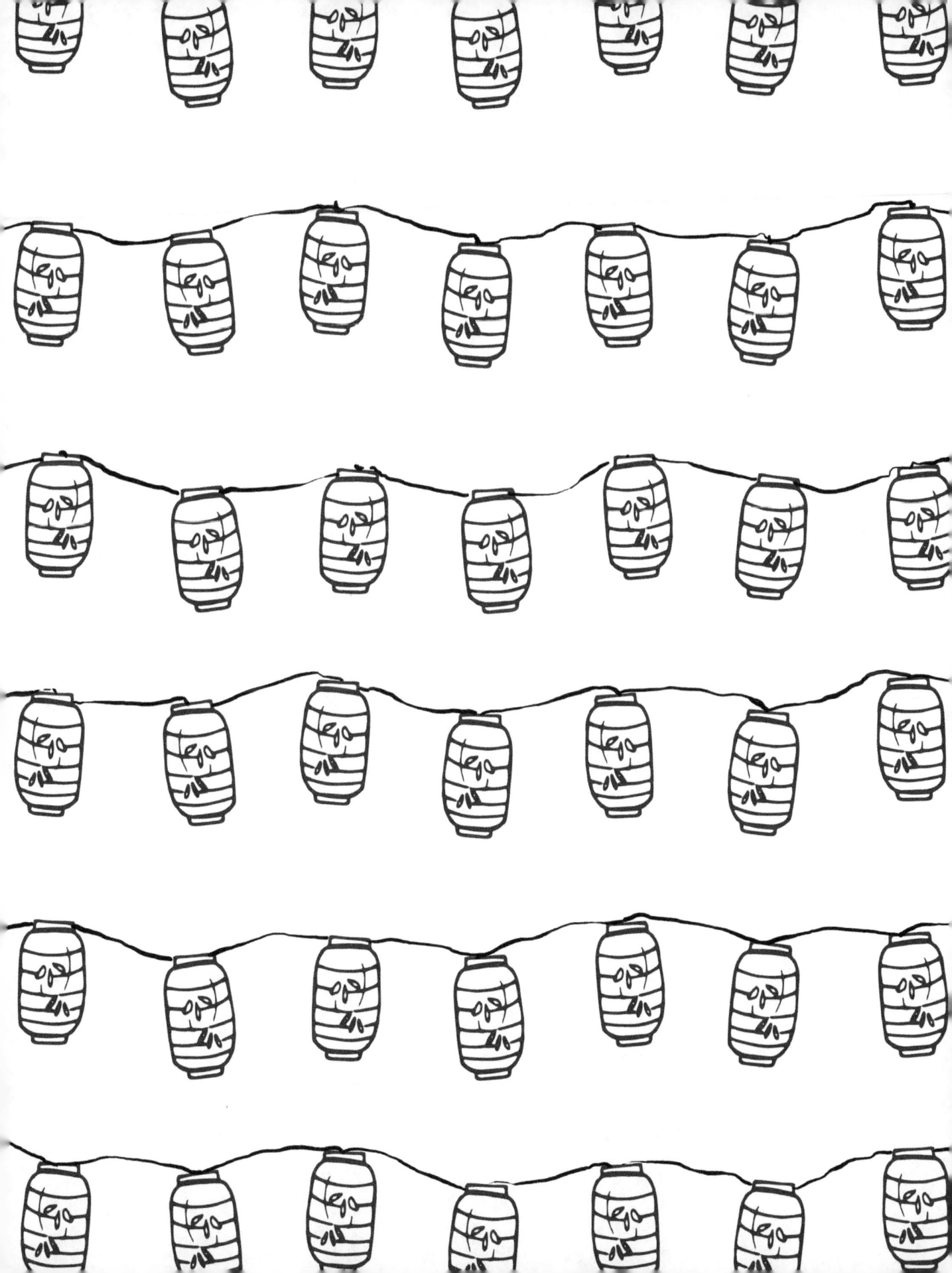

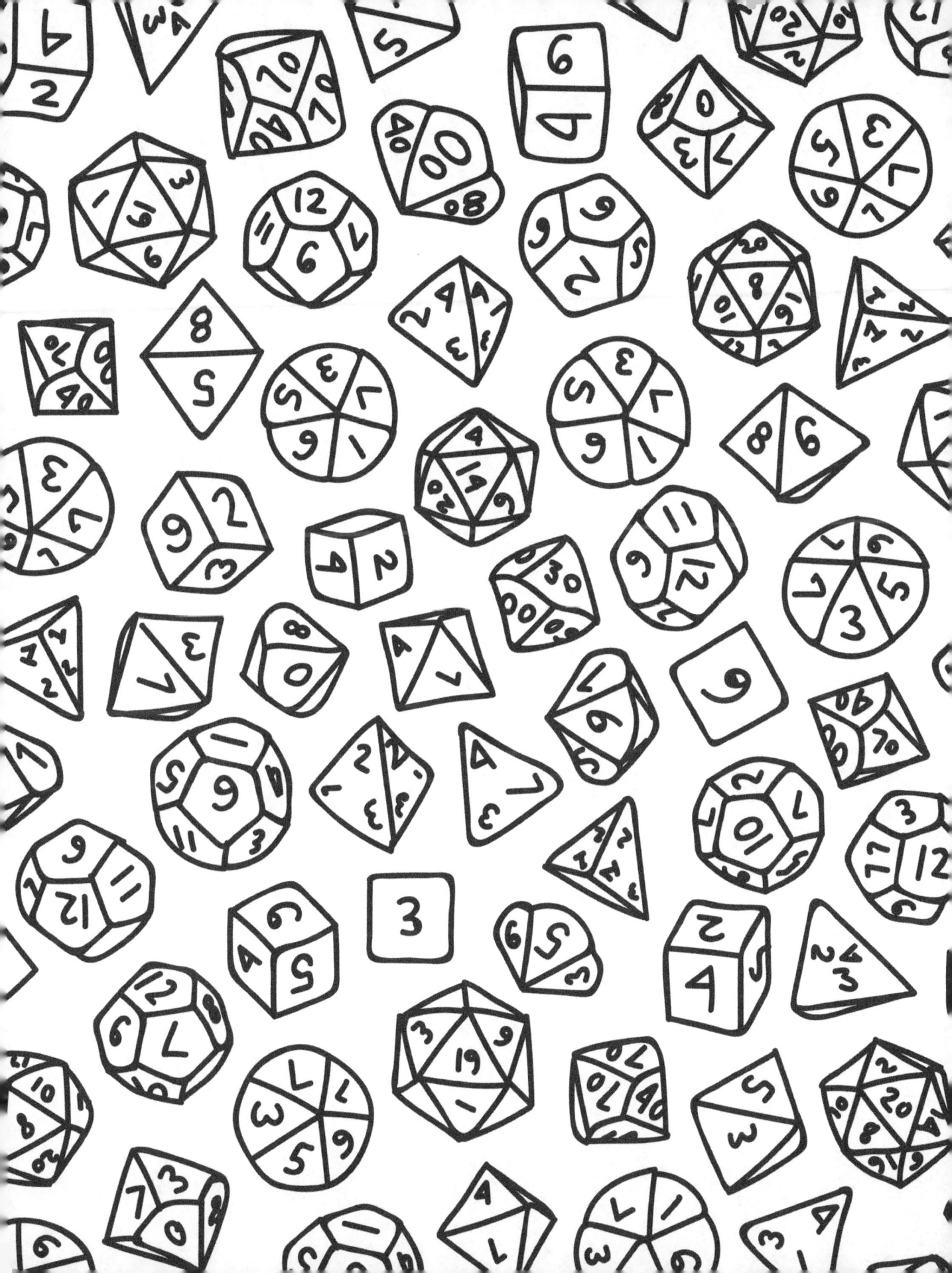

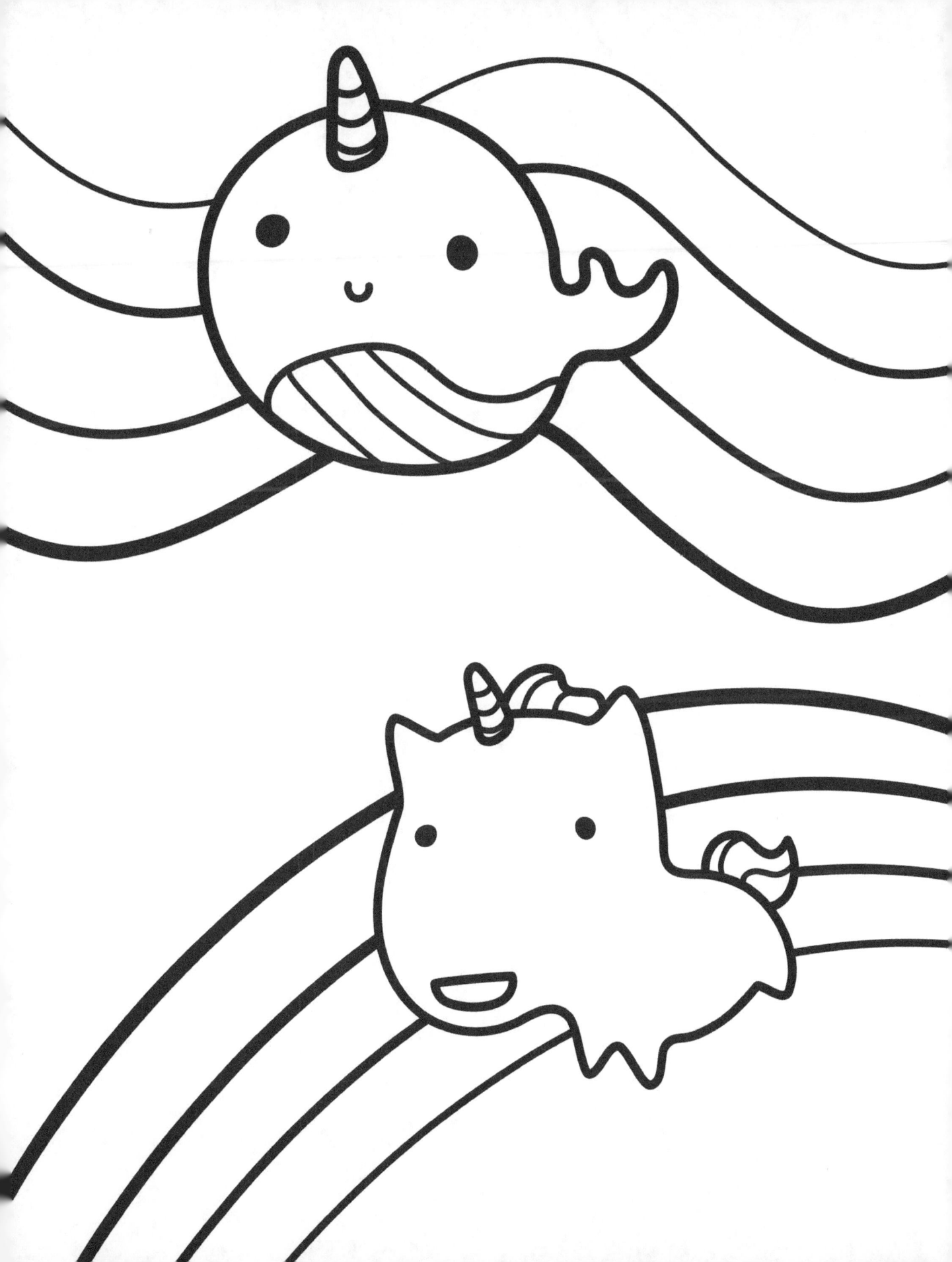

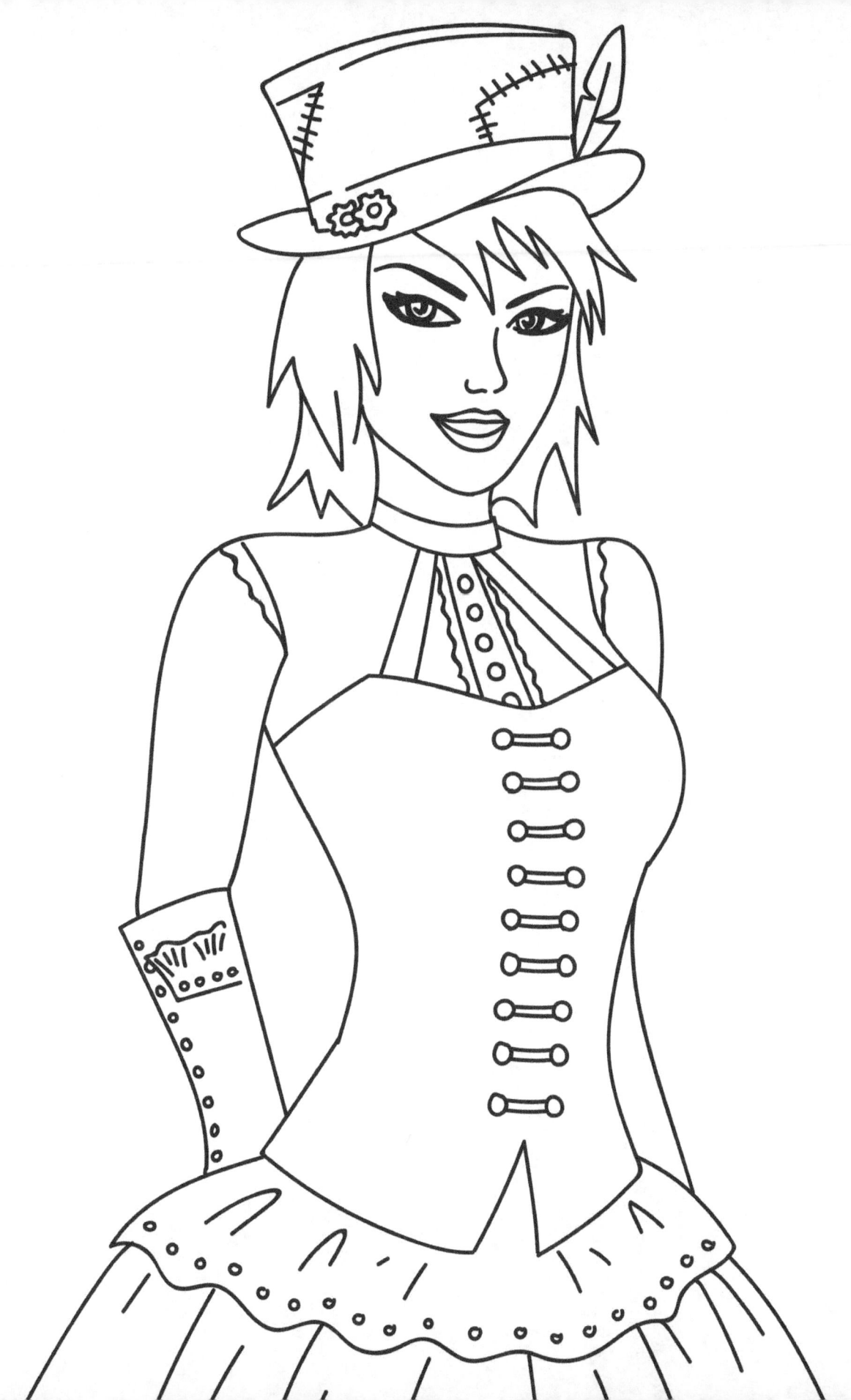

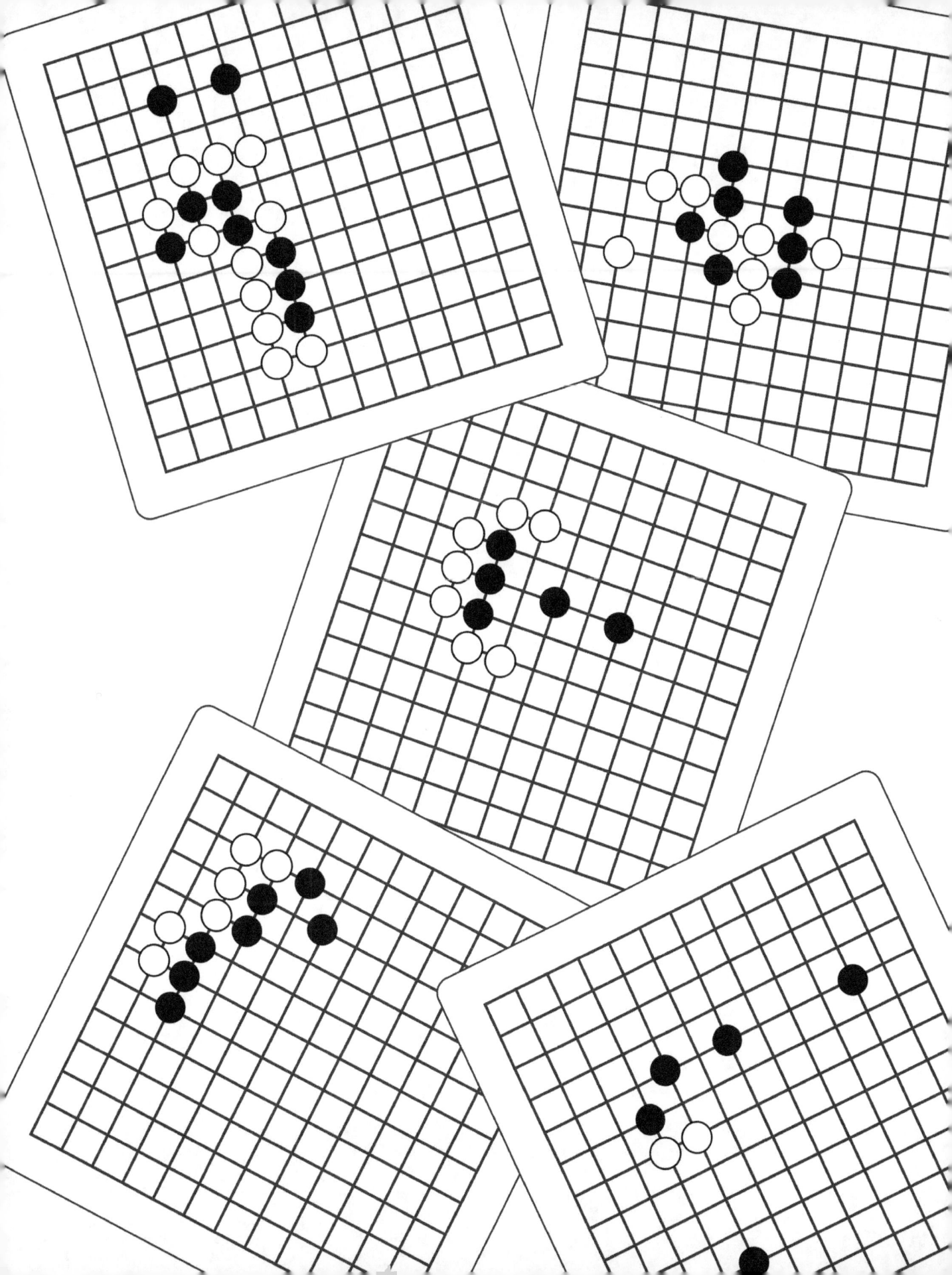

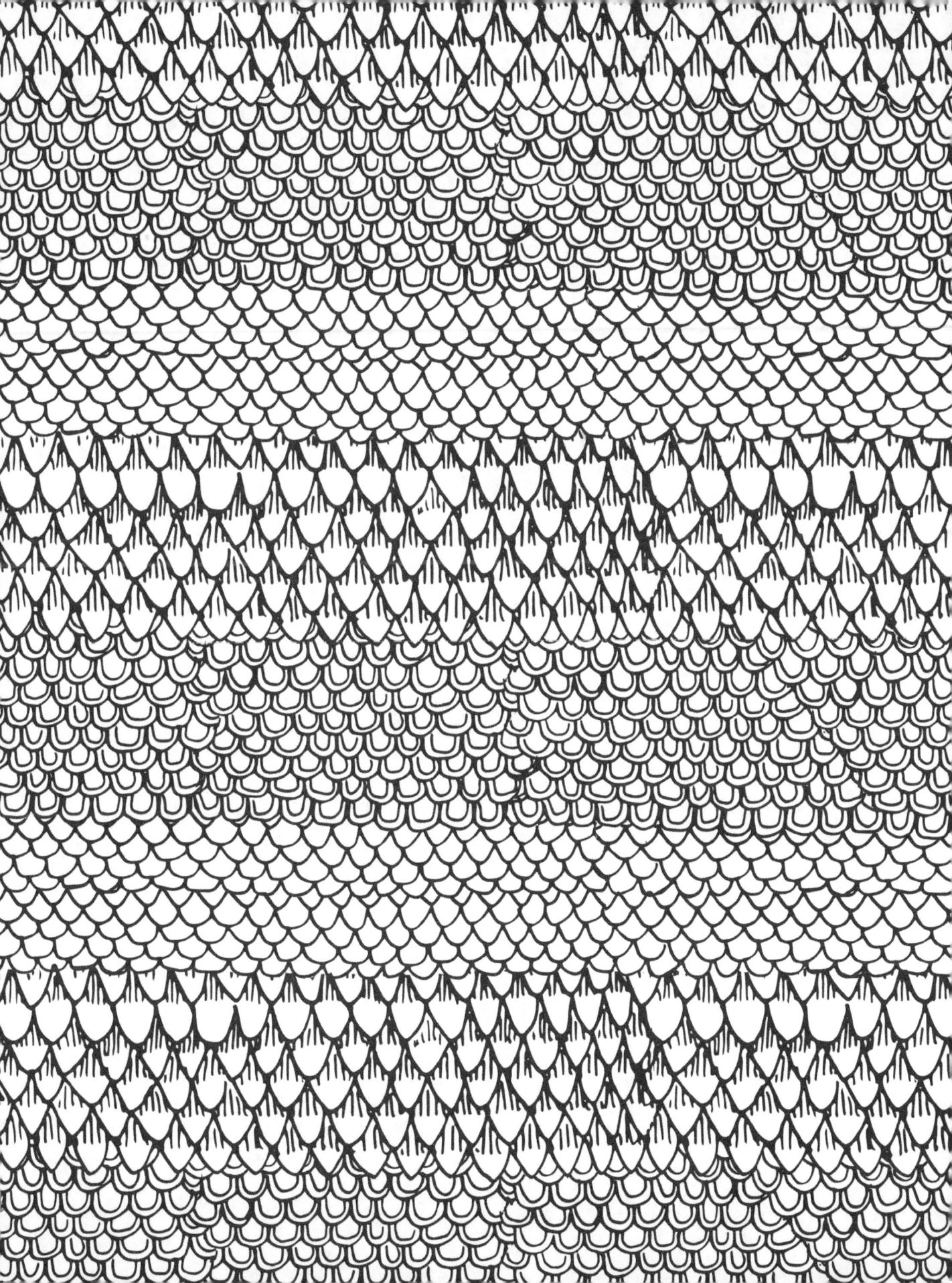

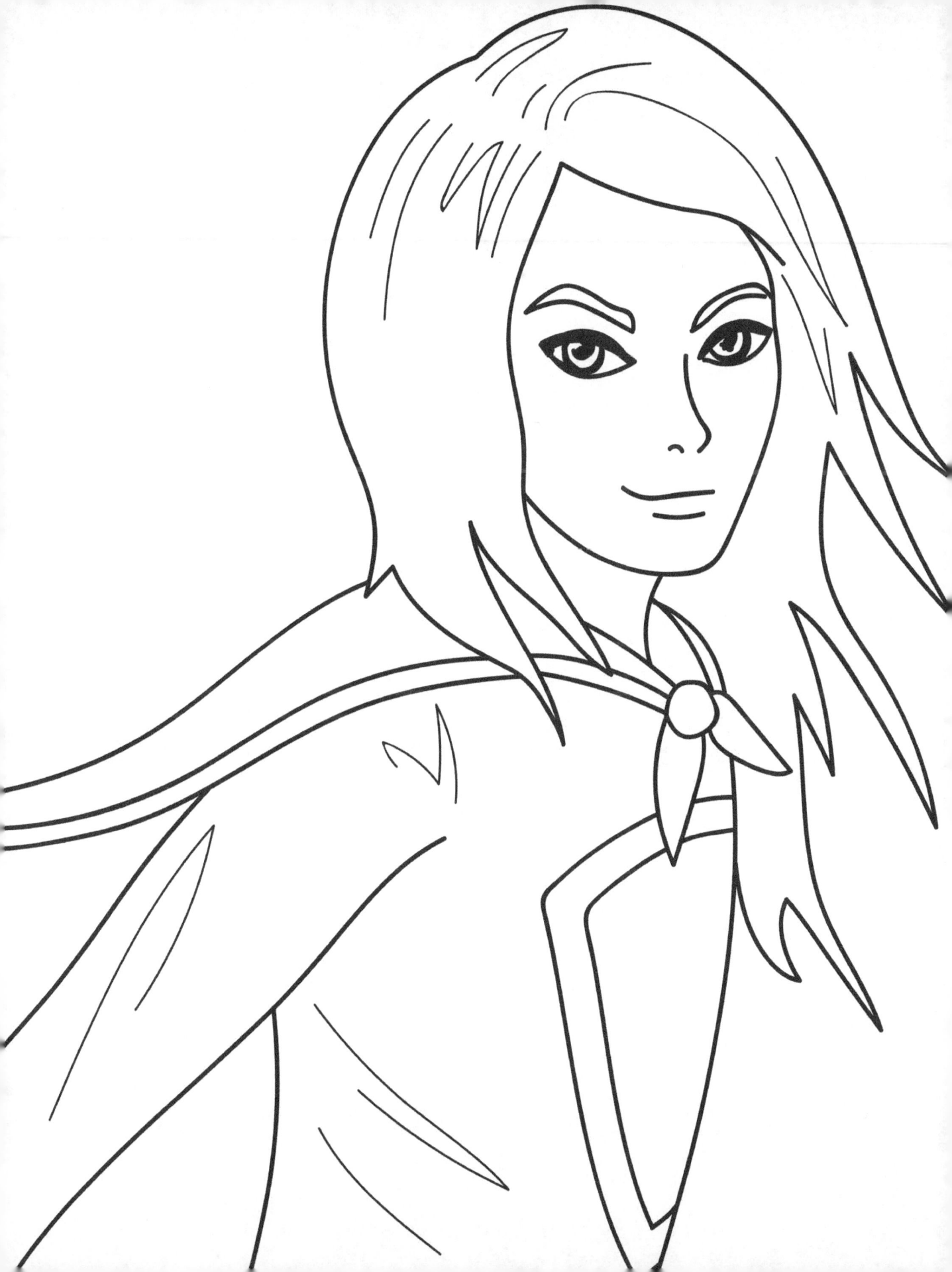

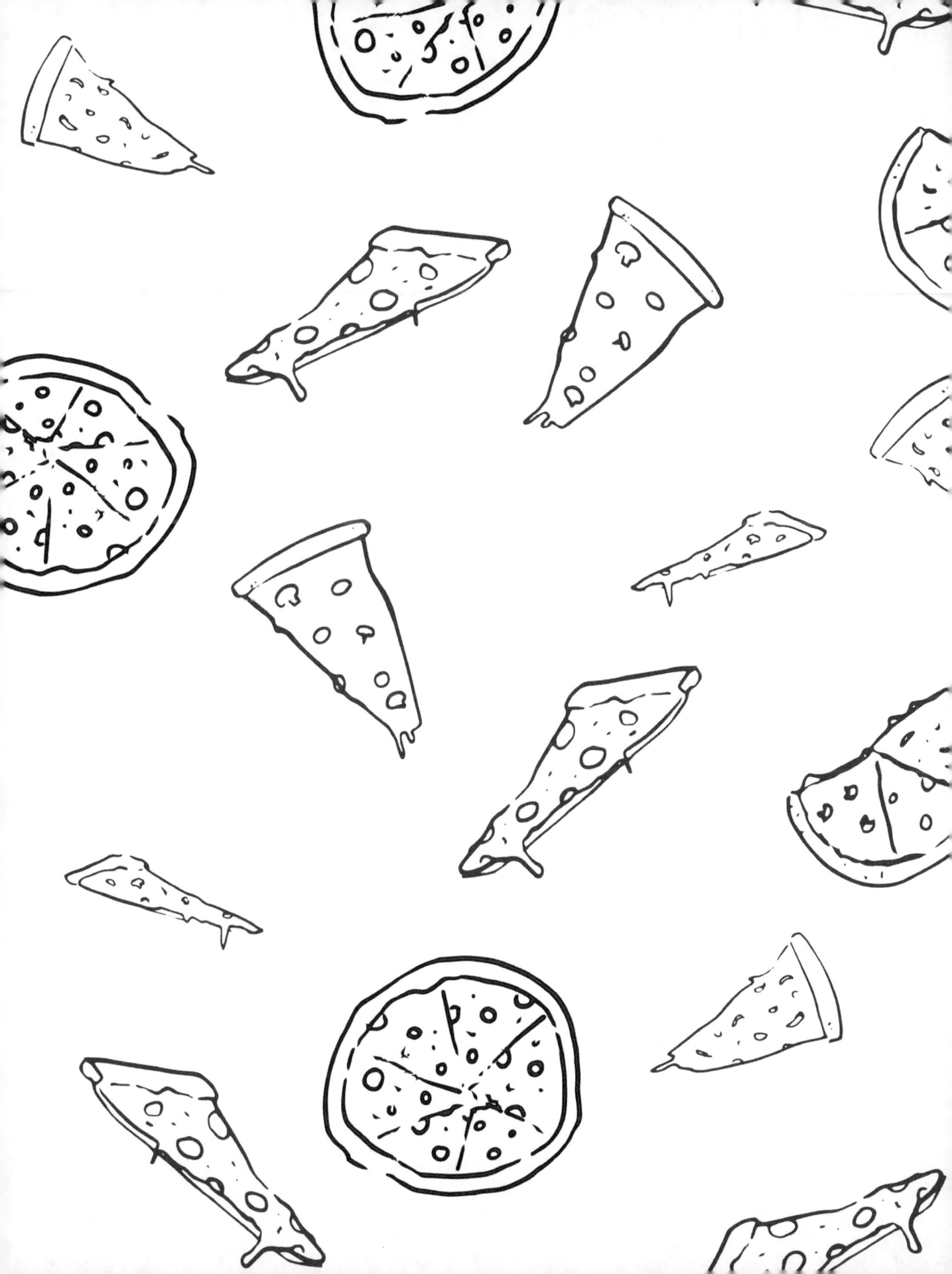

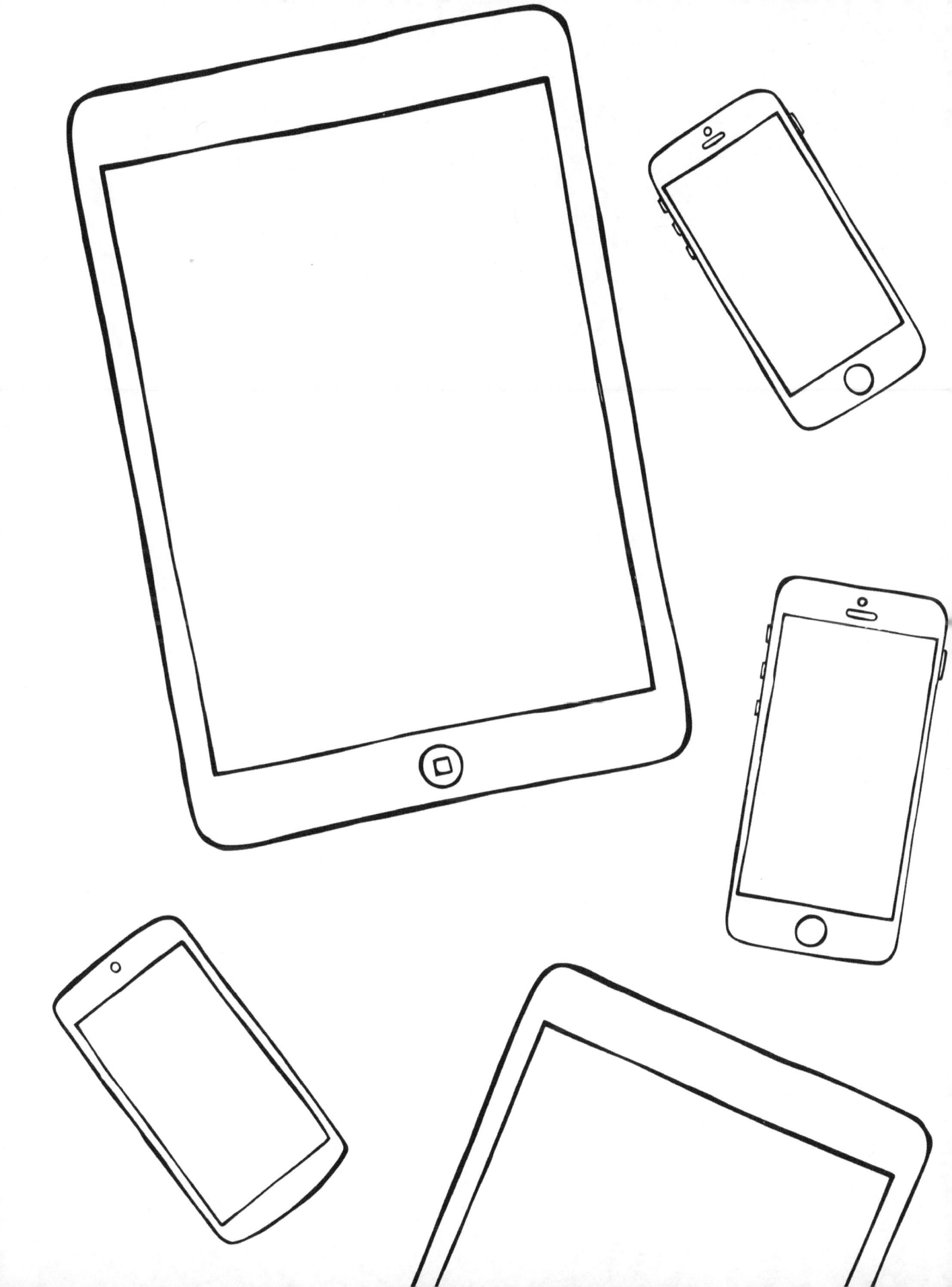

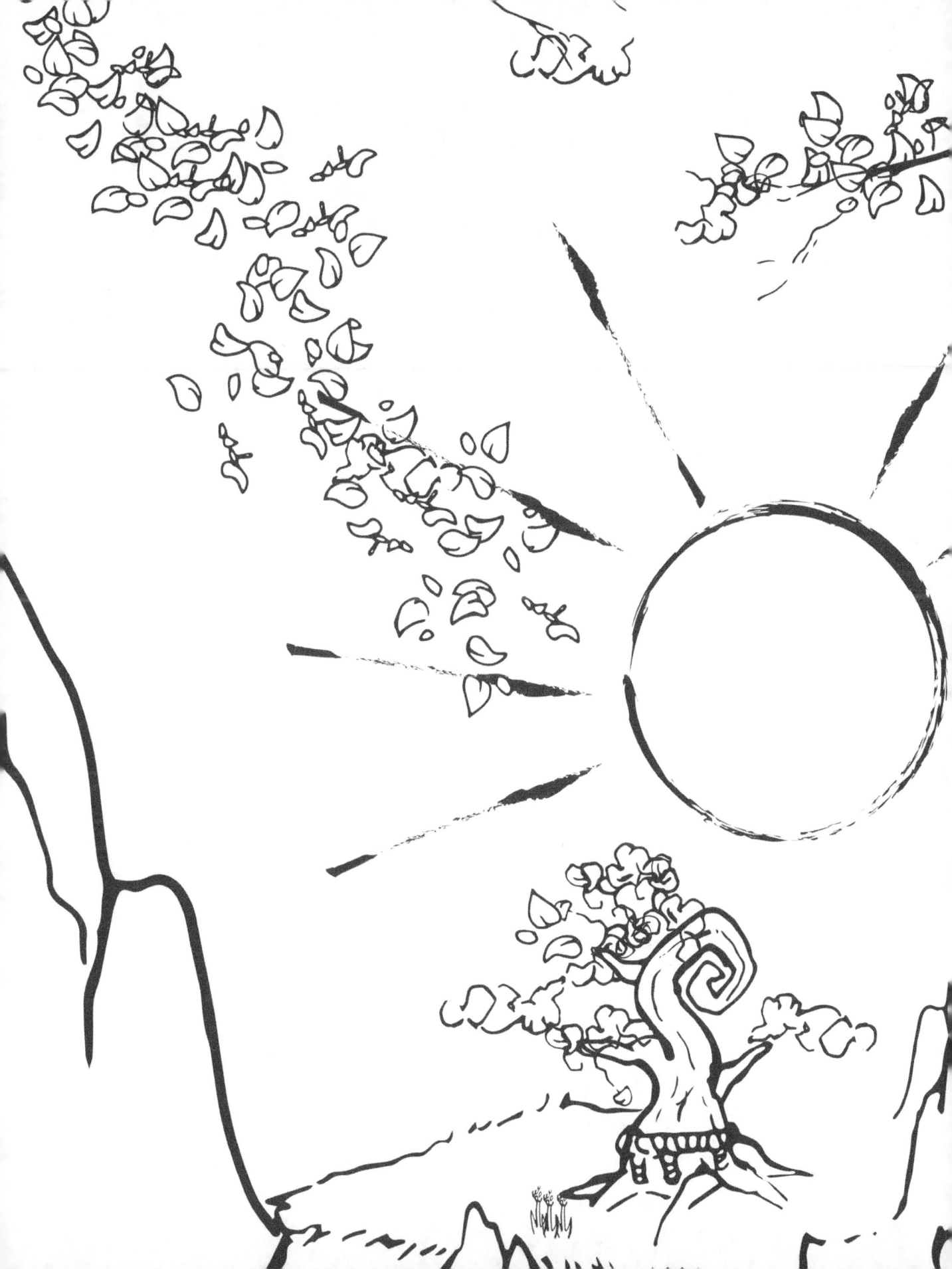

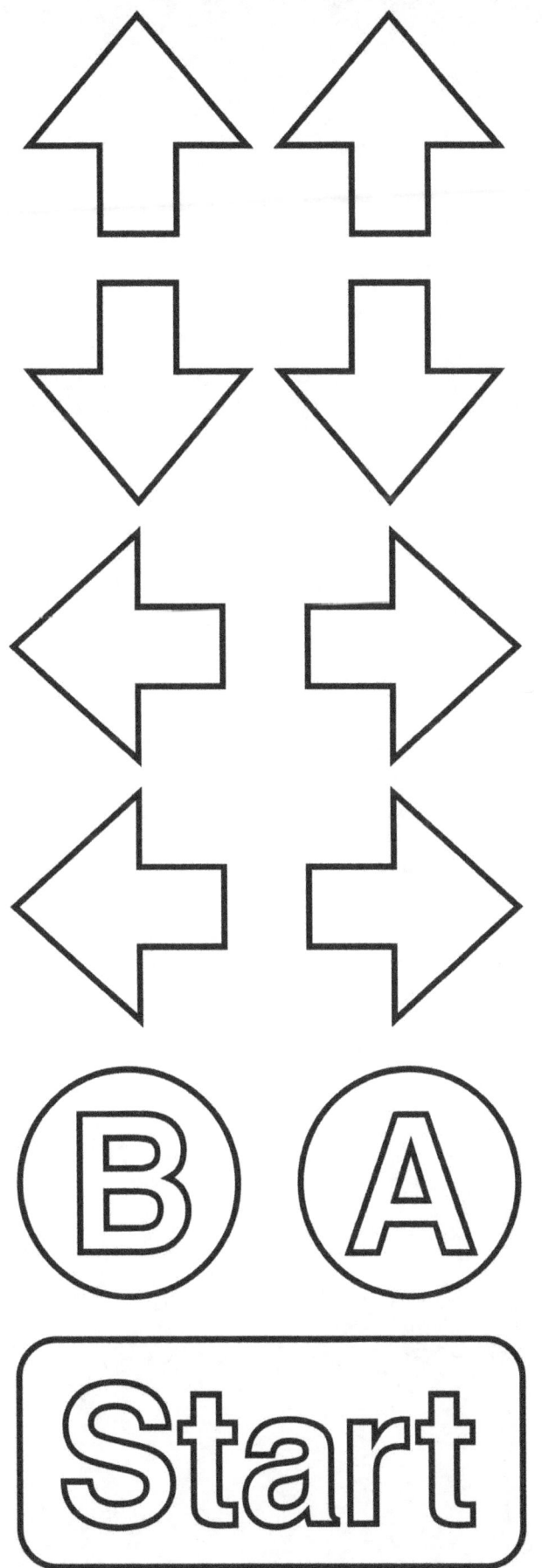

A Note From Our Authors...

This coloring book was a crazy thought during an awesome art night and we have some amazing people to thank for making it happen.

To our friends and family for your support in all our art endeavors - you constantly inspire and push us to do our best. Please don't ever stop doing that.

We also owe a special thanks to Brian and Kienan for your video game playing to help get us in the zone on all those art nights. Achaka!

And to our fanpersons of all ages, we love you!

xoxo
Colleen and Jaleh

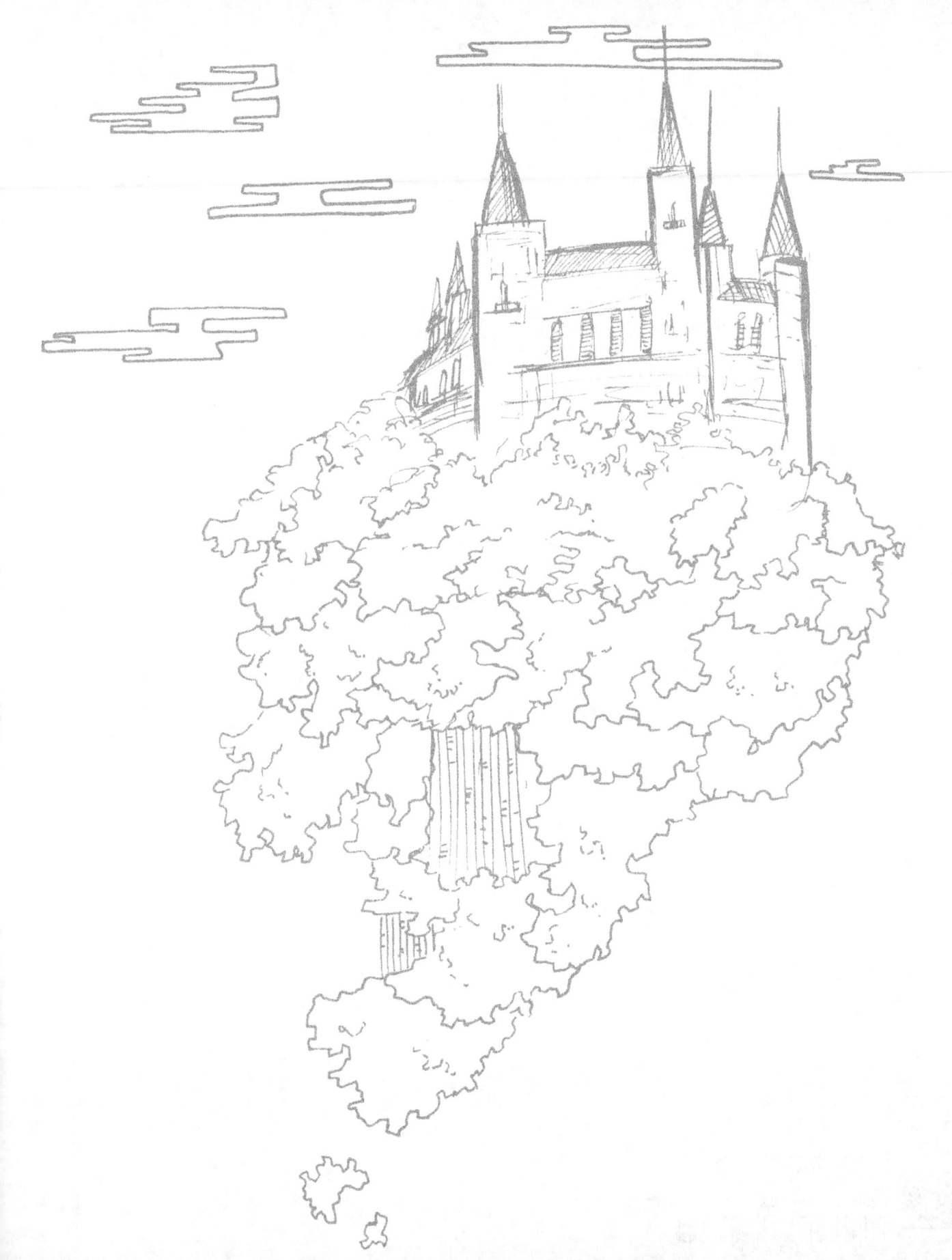

www.ingramcontent.com/pod-product-compliance
Lightning Source LLC
Chambersburg PA
CBHW080625190526
45169CB00009B/3288